Berlitz®

SPAIN

- A ☑ in the text denotes a highly recommended sight
- A complete A–Z of practical information starts on p.149
- Extensive mapping throughout: on cover flaps and in text

Although we make every effort to ensure the accuracy of the information in this guide, changes do occur. If you have any new information, suggestions or corrections to contribute, we would like to hear from you. Please write to Berlitz Publishing at one of the above addresses.

Text:	Emma Stanford
Editors:	Jack Messenger, Renée Ferguson
Photography:	Berlitz Publishing Co. Ltd except: Jon Davison 117-121, 135; Dany Ginoux 30, 34, 37, 39; Claude Huber 6, 9, 17, 20, 40-42, 55-66, 71-80, 82, 83, 85, 101, 115, 140; Paul Murphy 11-16, 46, 48, 51, 99, 102, 104 (bottom), 106, 110, 114, 122-129, 131, 142-146; Neil Wilson 84, 87, 89, 92, 98, 108, 111, 112, 134, 133, 137, 141.
Layout:	Suzanna Boyle
Cartography:	Visual Image

Thanks to: Ken Bernstein, Paul Murphy and the Spanish National Tourist Office for their assistance in the preparation of this book.

Front cover: *La Mancha*, Claude Huber
Back cover: *Seville orange tree*, Neil Wilson
Photograph on page 4: *Marbella*

CONTENTS

The Country and the People

From the rugged, mountainous Pyrenean border with France, west along the Bay of Biscay to the vast Atlantic Ocean, and south to the sunny Mediterranean coast, Spain occupies the lion's share of the Iberian peninsula, pushing neighbouring Portugal into a long, narrow strip along its western edge. After France and Russia, it is the third largest country in Europe. Physically and culturally diverse, the nation holds enormous appeal for both the adventurous traveller and dedicated sunseeker.

Beyond the famous *costas*, beautiful cities, fine palaces and imposing fortresses bear testimony to a rip-roaring history of Moorish invaders and New World *conquistadores*, introspective kings and ambitious emperors. On and off the beaten track, there is spectacular scenery and a host of hidden delights including the tiny fishing villages that cling like limpets to the wave-lashed *rías* of Galicia and Andalusia's whitewashed hill towns, asleep among the olive groves.

Although it forms part of continental Europe, the history of Spain has developed independently from mainstream European affairs. The 8th-century Moorish invasions from North Africa, just 14km (9 miles) across the Straits of Gibraltar, has lent a distinctive flavour to Spanish culture and tradition still apparent today. Threatened by only one neighbour with expansionist ideas, namely France, Spain managed to escape instant involvement in numerous European conflicts over the centuries.

Regionally, the country is deeply divided and has no less than three semi-autonomous regions in the north – Catalonia, the Basque Country and Galicia, all of which speak their own languages. Castilian is spoken throughout the rest of the country (and understood elsewhere), but the local people, along with their surroundings, differ widely in custom and character – from the hardy

*F*lamenco dancers celebrate the annual gypsy pilgrimage of El Rocio in Andalusia.

mountain men of Navarre to the fiery Andalusian.

After a relatively quiet period in the 1970s and 1980s, during which time the dictator Franco was buried and his successor, King Juan Carlos, was installed along with a new democratic constitution, Spain has launched into the 1990s in top gear. The 500th anniversary of Christopher Columbus' voyage to the New World was marked by the 1992 Olympic Games in Barcelona, Expo '92 in Seville, and by Spain gaining full economic partner status in the European Union.

Though parts of the old industrialized northern sector are suffering post-industrial blues, Spain's economy as a whole is strong (few bargains for visitors in currency exchange) and the prognosis is healthy. This economic confidence has done wonders for quality control, resulting in a huge change in standards of general facilities ranging from shopping and services to highways and hotel accommodation. But these improvements have prompted a significant increase in prices since the days when Spain was the bargain sunspot of Europe. Still, it is worth every *peseta*.

Where to Begin – A Bird's Eye View

Spain is so big (504,880sq km/194,885sq miles) there is no way you can 'do' it in a fortnight. It is best to select an area that appeals to you or, if you're not sure, to explore a region at a time and really get a feel for the land and its people. The obvious starting point is Madrid, the Spanish capital and transport hub at the geographical heart of the country. A bustling metropolis with a population of around 4 million, Madrid offers visitors elegant buildings and museums galore, including the incomparable Prado Museum, a 'must' on any art lover's itinerary.

To the north and within easy reach of the capital, lies Philip II's brooding Escorial Palace and the golden stone city of Segovia. Due south, touristy but delightful, is Toledo – a treasure-house of fine arts and the religious centre of Spain.

Another excellent place to launch your trip is Barcelona, Spain's second largest city and capital of Catalonia. Dynamic, prosperous and proudly Catalan, Barcelona's top attractions include a medieval Gothic quarter and the inspired creations of Moderniste architect Antoni Gaudí, as well as great nightlife and good food.

The Heart of the Country

North and west of Madrid, on Spain's high, central plateau (*La Meseta*), a quartet of fine old Castilian cities recall the 15th- and 16th-century Golden Age of Spain: handsome Salamanca; León and Burgos in the north; and Valladolid.

To the east, the wine-growing region of La Rioja is a hospitable corner of Spain. South of Madrid, the windmills and dramatic, wide open spaces of Don Quixote's La Mancha shimmer in the high heat. Late spring and early autumn are **7**

good times to visit the central region, bearing in mind the old Spanish weather warning of 'nine months of winter, three months of hell'.

Green Spain and the North

The three provinces on the north coast: Galicia, Asturias and Cantabria receive up to six times the average rainfall of parched La Mancha – hence the name. Here, the vines and orchards are heavy with fruit, and the July-August holiday season sees Spanish families flock to the sandy beaches of **8** the Atlantic seashore.

Galicia's charms include the lovely pilgrim town of Santiago de Compostela. Asturias and Cantabria offer a selection of hiking and climbing routes in the spectacular Picos de Europa mountains, plus appealing towns and seaside resorts.

At the far corner of the north coast, the Basque Country (*Euskadi*) climbs from the sea into the Pyrenees. Here, the complex Basque language adorns jaunty little fishing

boats and road signs in an unpronounceable welter of Xs, Ks and Zs, while Basque cooking is rated as some of the tastiest in Spain.

The Camino de Santiago, an ancient pilgrim passage from France to the shrine of St James at Santiago de Compostela, begins in the mountains of neighbouring Navarre, and passes through Pamplona.

To the east, the northern portion of Aragon has one foot

Tilting at almond trees (left) proves more fruitful than tilting at windmills (above).

in the Pyrenees and the other dipped in the Ebro, Spain's largest river. Here, the provincial capital of Zaragoza boasts the superb Aljafería – a Moorish palace unrivalled by any other outside Andalusia.

'España por favor' and the Wild West

Home of flamenco and bull-fighting, Andalusia is the Spain of the familiar travel office poster. Here, the Moorish strongholds of Granada and Córdoba form two corners of a triangular inland tourist route with the delightful Andalusian capital of Seville.

North of Andalusia, along the western border with Portugal, the harsh, arid landscape of Extremadura is as challenging as it is striking. The Romans left their mark here at Mérida, but it is in medieval Cáceres and Trujillo that one finds traces of the *conquistadores*, natives of this hardbitten region, who brought home the spoils of the New World to enrich their churches.

Cream of the Costas

The pick of the Spanish beaches begins below the Mediterranean border with France. The sandy coves and cliffs of the Costa Brava mark the eastern end of the Pyrenees. South of Barcelona, the *costas Azahar* (Orange Blossom), *Dorada* (Gold), *Blanca* (White), *Cálida* (Warm) and *Almería* (unimaginatively named for its chief town), hug the Mediterranean all the way around to the southern Costa del Sol. Here, both princes and package tourists lay equal claim to their place in the sun, while visitors to the windy Costa de la Luz on the Atlantic coast had better hang on to their towels. The Atlantic and northern Mediterranean beaches are essentially summer season playgrounds, but the Costa del Sol never sleeps and attracts visitors throughout the year.

Islands in the Sun

Off Spain's eastern Mediterranean coast, the Balearic Islands of Majorca and Minorca still manage to keep a few relatively unexplored corners for independent travellers. The hip island of Ibiza throbs to the disco-party beat all summer long, whereas the more beach-orientated Formentera makes for an effective rest cure.

Visitors from the northern hemisphere in search of serious winter sunshine and swimming need look no further than the Canary Islands. Anchored off the coast of Africa, these seven Spanish islands vary in appearance from towering Tenerife to flat-as-a-pancake Fuerteventura. The two other most frequented holiday islands in the group are Gran Canaria and Lanzarote.

Something for Everyone

The sheer size and variety of scenery in Spain really does mean that there is something here to attract everyone. You'll gain most from your stay in the country if you try not to do too much. Each of the semi-autonomous regions of Spain offers a wealth of distinct cultural and scenic delights, so immerse yourself and enjoy!

A place in the sun: soaking up golden rays on Spain's Mediterranean coast.

11

A Brief History

Spain's history is as rugged and colourful as the land itself. It is a tale of Moorish domination and a glorious Golden Age; of empires and colonies conquered and defeated; brave knights and foolish kings; and a bloody and destructive Civil War which saw Spain excommunicated from the international community for some three decades of the 20th century. Yet, almost unbelievably, twenty years post-Franco, the rehabilitation of Spain is more than complete.

Early History

The earliest inhabitants of the Iberian peninsula were Paleolithic people who probably arrived via a land bridge linking Europe and Africa between Gibraltar and Morocco. As Europe moved into the Ice Age, the first Spaniards put on their bearskin coats, stoked up their fires and fed off deer, bison and wild horses – just like those depicted on the walls and ceilings of caves discovered in Cantabria, near Altamira, which date back at least 15,000 years.

During the Bronze Age, Celtic immigrants settled in northern and central Spain, while the south and east were inhabited by various Iberian tribes of North African origin. The Iberians had their own written language, sophisticated industry and tools, and they created fine artworks such as the stone sculpture of a goddess, known as *La Dama de Elche* (The Lady of Elche), a star attraction at Madrid's Archaeological Museum. The Celts and the Iberians interacted where their territories overlapped and developed a distinct Celtiberian culture for which the Celts supplied the brawn, and the Iberians the brains. The Celtiberians soon gained fame as soldiers and it is said that they invented the two-edged warrior's sword (later to become standard equipment in the Roman army, and to be used against them).

In the meanwhile, Phoenicians, sailing from bases in

Historical Landmarks

3,000BC	Bronze Age: Celts settle in north; Iberians in south.
1,100BC	Phoenicians found Gadir (Cádiz).
3rd cen. BC	Carthaginians conquer much of Spain.
1st cen. BC	Romans complete conquest of Spain.
1st cen. AD	Christianity introduced.
4th cen.	Decline of Roman Empire.
6th cen.	Visigoths make Toledo their capital.
711	Moors invade Andalusia; and control most of Spain.
722	Christian victory of the Reconquest at Covadonga.
758	Córdoba becomes Moorish capital.
1474	Ferdinand of Aragon marries Isabella of Castile.
1478	Inauguration of the Inquisition.
1492	Reconquest. Expulsion of Jews. Columbus' voyage.
1516	Charles I inherits Spanish throne.
1556-98	Philip II rules from Madrid.
1588	Defeat of Spanish Armada.
1618-48	Thirty Years' War.
1701-14	War of Spanish Succession. Philip V wins the crown.
1804-14	War of Independence. Ferdinand VII regains throne.
1833-76	Internal strife: Carlist Wars.
1898	Spanish-American War: end of empire.
1914-18	Spain stays neutral in World War I; domestic unrest.
1923-30	Primo de Rivera's dictatorship supported by king.
1931	Anti-monarchist election victory; king chooses exile.
1936	Left-wing government elected. Start of Civil War.
1939	Republicans defeated; Franco in power.
1975	Franco dies; King Juan Carlos accedes. Democracy.
1986	Spain joins EU.
1992	Olympic Games, Barcelona; Seville hosts Expo '92.

Romans in the Second Punic War. This left the way open for Rome to take control of the peninsula, though it took nearly 200 years to subjugate the stubborn Celtiberians.

Spain under the Caesars

Second to the homeland itself, Spain was to become the most important part of the Roman Empire. All over the country, the stamp of Roman civilization remains in walls and roadways, villas, monuments and vineyards. Three living Spanish languages are descended from Latin: Gallego (Galician) Castilian and Catalan. Roman law forms the foundation of the Spanish legal system, and Spain gave birth to Roman emperors as memorable as Trajan and Hadrian, as well as the writers Seneca and Martial.

North Africa, founded several colonies in southern Spain. The first of these, founded in about 1100BC, was Gadir (present-day Cadiz). Carthage, which was itself a Phoenician colony, established an empire of its own that spread as far north into Spain as Barcelona. The profit-seeking Carthaginians exploited Spain's silver and lead mines and drafted the country's young, able-bodied males into their army.

During the 3rd century BC, the Carthaginian forces under Hannibal were defeated by the

The Romans divided the peninsula into two: *Hispaniae Ulterior* and *Hispaniae Citerior* ('farther' and 'nearer' respectively). When it was later carved into three provinces, the capital cities were established at what are now Mérida (Extremadura), Córdoba (Andalusia) and Tarragona (Catalonia). Christianity came to Spain early in the Roman period. The word may have been carried by St Paul himself (he is said to have preached both in Aragon and at Tarragona). However, the Christian community suffered considerable persecution.

The Visigoths

Overstretched and increasingly corrupt, Rome watched its far-flung colonies disintegrate. Germanic tribes, some with a deserved reputation for barbarism, hastened into the vacuum. The Vandals had little to contribute to Spanish culture. However, the Gaulish Visigoths from France did bring a certain constructive influence. Former allies of Rome, they ruled from Toledo, where they displayed their intricate arts and built opulent churches.

The 300-year regime of the Visigoths never achieved any measure of national unity, and eventually foundered on the thorny question of succession. The commendably democratic principle of elective monarchy fostered a web of intrigue and assassination as contenders attempted to secure the crown. These, as well as other problems, were often blamed on the handiest scapegoat: the industrious and successful Jews. They had fared well under the Romans and early Visigoths, but at the start of the 7th century non-Christians were forced either to convert to Catholicism or face exile.

Enter the Moors

During AD711, an invited expeditionary force of around 12,000 Berber troops from North Africa sailed across the Straits of Gibraltar and poured ashore into Spain. The expertly planned invasion was led by General Tariq ibn Ziyad (the **15** name 'Gibraltar' is a corruption of *Gibel Tariq* – Tariq's Rock). His ambition was to spread the influence of Islam.

Within just three years, the Moors or *moros* (as North African Muslims are usually called in Spanish history) had reached the Pyrenees. Due in

A sturdy 16th-century watchtower surveys the town of Vilassar de Mar.

part to the Visigoths' military disorganization, the Moors' initial success was also assisted by ordinary citizens attracted to promises of lower taxes and a chance of freedom for serfs. Spanish Jews welcomed the Moors as liberators as, initially at least, the occupation stipulated religious tolerance. However, conversion to Islam was thoroughly encouraged, and many Christians chose to embrace the Muslim creed.

The most tangible relics of this time are now among Spain's greatest tourist attractions: the exquisite Moorish palaces and mosques of Córdoba, Granada and Seville. Thanks to the irrigation techniques imported from North Africa, crops like rice, cotton and sugar were planted, and orchards of almonds, pomegranates, oranges and peaches thrived. Other Moorish innovations made possible the production of paper and glass, and the art of medieval Moorish artisans is preserved in today's best Spanish craft buys – ceramics, tooled leather and intricate silverwork.

The Spanish Strike Back

The Moorish juggernaut that trundled north from Gibraltar in 711 met no serious resistance. It was eleven years before the fragmented defenders of Christian Spain won their first battle. Exiled to the northern territory of Asturias, the Visigoth nobles, led by Pelayo, joined with local mountain folk to strike the first blow for the Reconquest (or *Reconquista*). Further Christian victories would be a long time coming, but Pelayo's success at the Battle of Covadonga (the village is now a shrine) gave heart to a struggle that was to simmer for centuries.

In the middle of the 8th century, the Christians of Asturias, under King Alfonso I, took advantage of a rebellion by Berber troops to occupy neighbouring Galicia. Here, at Santiago de Compostela, the alleged discovery of the tomb of the apostle St James (Santiago) was to become the religious focal point for Spanish Christians and a rallying call

*D*ressed to kill: Moorish-Christian battles are re-enacted at Alcoy (Alicante).

to defenders of the Christian faith throughout Europe. More breathing space from Moorish pressure was won in what became Catalonia. Charlemagne, King of the Franks, established a buffer zone between Islamic Spain and France, south of the Pyrenees, and captured Barcelona. Spanish **17**

Christians then seized the advantage and expanded south and west into the area between Catalonia and Asturias, which soon had so many frontier castles it was called Castile.

The Reconquest see-sawed on for hundreds of years, as each side gained and lost political advantage and military initiative under a succession of leaders. Over the centuries, squabbles amongst the Moors resulted in alliances of convenience with the Christians, and

the intermingling of the two cultures was commonplace. Christians who thrived in the Moorish regions, known as *Mozárabes*, and the Moorish inhabitants of Christian enclaves (*Mudéjars*) gave their names to the two most important art styles of this period.

Early in the 10th century, the Asturian capital was transferred approximately 120km (75 miles) south from Oviedo to León, a symbolic step deep into former 'infidel' territory.

El Cid

The legend of El Cid, Spain's national folk hero, is recounted in the epic poem, *El cantar de mío Cid*. Born Rodrigo Díaz de Vivar, near Burgos in around 1040, he was a highly successful soldier of fortune. Vivar at first fought for the kings of Castile in the battle against the Moors. When Sancho II died in mysterious circumstances, Vivar humiliated his successor, Alfonso VI, by forcing him to swear publicly that he had nothing to do with Sancho's death. Exiled for his impudence, Vivar joined the Moors, from whom he received his honorary title, El Cid (Arabic for 'Lord'). El Cid's greatest victory was in 1094, when he led a Christian-Moorish army to take Valencia, where he died in 1099. Encouraged by his death, a Moorish army regrouped to take the city. El Cid's body was propped on his horse and ridden before the defending army which routed the attackers.

However the Muslims were far from on the run. United under the dictator al-Mansur ('the victorious'), they reclaimed León, Barcelona, Burgos and, in a severe blow to Christian morale, sacked the town of Santiago de Compostela. The death of the charismatic al-Mansur in 1002 revived Christian hopes. In 1010, they succeeded in recapturing al-Mansur's headquarters of Córdoba, and the city of Toledo fell in 1085.

The fall of Toledo sent out shock waves to Moorish rulers elsewhere in Spain and they called for help from the Almoravids, a North African confederation of puritanical Muslim Berber tribes based in Marrakesh. Known for their military prowess, they halted

Religious art – both Christian and Muslim – flourished during the Reconquest.

19

The Jewish community of Gerona played a significant role in the city's medieval prosperity.

the Reconquest, but in the 12th century sent for further reinforcements from the Almohad fundamentalists, who stepped up the persecution of Jews and *Mozárabes*. The turning point of the Reconquest is held to be the Battle of Las Navas de Tolosa in 1212. In its wake, the Christian forces regained most

of Spain south to Andalusia, the point where the final Moorish stronghold at Granada was recaptured in 1492.

A Singular Nation

Up until the 15th century, the various regional kingdoms of Spain remained resolutely independent. There were some sporadic moves towards unity, which usually involved strategic marriage contracts, and it was one such royal marriage which united the shrewd Ferdinand of Aragon and strongly religious and patriotic Isabella of Castile. Under the Catholic Monarchs (as Pope Alexander VI entitled them), a single Spain was created, comprising most of the nation we know today, though the component parts of the newly united kingdom retained their individuality and institutions.

Aiming to further unite the country, Ferdinand and Isabella inaugurated the Inquisition in 1478. Initially intended to safeguard religious orthodoxy under Isabella's influential confessor, the fanatical Tomás de Torquemada, it became a byword for the persecution of Jews, Muslims and later Protestants. Several thousand suspected heretics were horribly tortured and many publically burned at *autos-da-fé* (show trials). In 1492, Torquemada convinced Ferdinand and Isabella to expel the surviving unconverted Jews – perhaps 200,000 in all, including some of the country's best-educated and most productive citizens.

The year 1492 was a momentous one for Spanish history. Not only did it witness the expulsion of the Moors and the Jews, but also Europe's discovery of the New World by Genoese explorer Christopher Columbus. Sponsored by Queen Isabella (who, according to legend, pawned her own jewels to raise the money), the expedition and subsequent annexation of the New World territories laid the foundations for Spain's Golden Age.

The Habsburgs

While Ferdinand and Isabella were Spain personified, their grandson and heir to the throne, Charles I, born in Flanders in 1500, could barely compose a sentence in Spanish. Through his father, Philip, Duke of Burgundy, he inherited extensive possessions in the Low Countries; and he was appointed Holy Roman Emperor (Charles V) in 1519. An unpopular king, Charles alienated his Spanish subjects by appointing Flemish and Burgundian supporters in key posts such as Archbishop of Toledo and regent during his frequent absences. Charles' **21** expansionist foreign policies consolidated Burgundy and the Netherlands as Spanish provinces. He also annexed Milan and Naples and drew Spain into a series of costly European wars funded from the seemingly bottomless pit of Spain's New World bounty.

In 1556, overwhelmed by his responsibilities, Charles abdicated in favour of his son, Philip II. Born and educated in Spain, the new king gave top jobs to Castilians and proclaimed Madrid his capital, thereby converting an unimpressive town of 15,000 into the powerhouse of the greatest empire of the age. As literature and the arts flourished, Philip worked endlessly to administer his over-extended territories. He captured Portugal, and shared in the glory following the destruction of the Turkish fleet at Lepanto (1571). However, the destruction of the Spanish fleet in the disastrous Armada episode (1588), and the spiralling costs of maintaining the empire, eventually robbed Philip of his health and severely depleted the Spanish

The 18th-century splendour of the Churinguera brothers' Plaza Mayor in Salamanca.

treasury. He died in devout seclusion at El Escorial, the palace-monastery in the hills northwest of Madrid.

Though Spain was still the dominant force in Europe at Philip's death, the Golden Age and empire were on the wane. Philip III delegated his responsibilities to his favourites, involved Spain in the Thirty Years' War of Catholics fighting Protestants, and expelled the remaining *moriscos*, many of them farmers, precipitating an agricultural crisis.

The final century of the Habsburg era was a gradual, then rapid decline in Spanish fortunes. Ironically, in contrast to the severe loss of territorial possessions and despite the ravages of war, pestilence and famine, the beautiful work of Velázquez, Zurbarán, Murillo and Ribera celebrated the high point of Spanish art.

The last of the Spanish Habsburgs, Charles II, died without an heir in 1700. He willed his crown to the Duke of Anjou, grandson of France's Louis XIV, who claimed the title Philip V of Spain. Archduke Charles of Austria (another Habsburg) contested the claim, which sparked the War of the Spanish Succession, ended by the Treaty of Utrecht in 1713.

Bourbons on the throne

Philip V eventually secured the throne, but his diminishing empire was now shorn of Belgium, Luxembourg, Milan, Sicily and Sardinia. To add insult to injury, Britain snatched strategic Gibraltar. The most successful Spanish king of the 18th century, Charles III, recruited capable administrators, disbanded the Inquisition, invigorated the economy and paved the streets of Madrid. But Spain came increasingly under the power of France during the Bourbon period.

After the defeat of Franco-Spanish fleet by the British at the Battle of Trafalgar in 1805, Charles IV had to abdicate. Napoleon appointed his brother Joseph as José I, and the Spanish uprising resulted in **23** the Peninsula War (Spaniards call it the War of Independence). The French were finally ousted with the help of British troops led by the Duke of Wellington in 1814. Meanwhile, several of Spain's most valuable American colonies had taken advantage of her preoccupation to win their independence.

With a Bourbon Spanish king, Ferdinand VII, once again on the throne, Spain failed miserably to prosper. Political infighting, a repressive monarchy and anti-clerical revolts led to the domestic Carlist Wars. The century ended with another disaster as Cuba, Puerto Rico and the Philippines were lost in the Spanish-American War.

The Spanish Civil War

Spain escaped the horrors of World War I, watching the carnage from a position of neutrality. Alfonso XIII backed the dictatorship of General Miguel Primo de Rivera (1923-30), but went into exile (never to return) after anti-royalist forces won a landslide victory in the 1931 elections. The new Republic was riven with bitter ideological conflicts, particularly between the Left and Right. A left-wing victory in the 1936 elections, and the assassination of the Monarchist

The Civil War Memorial at Valle de los Caídos (Valley of the Fallen) outside Madrid.

leader, Calvo Sotelo, ignited nationalist and conservative fears of a Marxist revolution. Monarchists, clergy as well as the right-wing Falange organization united behind the Movimiento Nacional led by the war hero, General Francisco Franco. Meanwhile, a motley band of liberals, communists, socialists, and anarchists cast their lot with the newly elected Spanish government.

The inevitable outcome was the Civil War: three years of horrific bloodshed and destruction which claimed between 50,000 and 75,000 lives and gutted towns and cities as father fought son, and region battled against region. Franco emerged victorious, but Spain was shattered physically and emotionally.

The New Spain

Although he was sympathetic to the Axis powers during World War II, Franco opted for neutrality, and quietly began to rebuild Spain. The trains ran on time and the streets were safe again, but there was a heavy atmosphere of repression and economic recovery was slow. On Franco's death in 1975, his chosen successor was Juan Carlos de Bourbon, grandson of Alfonso XIII, who was crowned king of a constitutional monarchy, and has proved an able and popular helmsman on Spain's road to democracy.

Fundamental changes in the political landscape came thick and fast in the 1970s and 80s as the Falange was wound down, the Communist party legalized, and a degree of autonomy was granted to the regions of Catalonia, Euskadi (Basque) and Galicia. Today, as a member of the United Nations, NATO and the EU, Spain's long separation from the world and European mainstream is over.

The last few years have seen further remarkable changes in the world view of Spain, and in the national psyche. The former poor relation of Europe is economically strong, culturally vibrant and able to look ahead confidently to the challenges of the 21st century.

25

'Kilometre 0' in the country's highway system, and home to a statue depicting Madrid's coat-of-arms (a bear standing against a *madroño* tree).

A few blocks west, off Calle Mayor, is the **Plaza Mayor** (Main Square), a 17th-century architectural masterpiece. Its broad arcades surround a vast, traffic-free, cobbled rectangle, once used as the inner city showground where bullfights, pageants and even public executions took place. Today, an equestrian statue of Philip II surveys serried ranks of outdoor cafés and lively summer season festivals.

Continuing west on Calle Mayor, Plaza de la Villa juxtaposes stately 16th- and 17th-century buildings of differing style. These include the lovely **Casa de Cisneros**, which belongs to the ornate and delicate style of architecture known as plateresque (*platero* means silversmith), and the towering Habsburg-era **Ayuntamiento** (City Hall).

South of Plaza Mayor, Calle de Toledo leads past the **Catedral de San Isidro**, badly damaged during the Civil War, and on to **El Rastro**, site of the city's famous Sunday-morning flea market. Just to the north of here, the mid-18th century **Basílica de San Francisco el Grande** is very grand indeed. Dedicated to St Francis of Assisi, the 100-foot inner diameter of the basilica's dome is larger than that of St Paul's in London.

Calle de Bailén runs north from San Francisco, via Calle Mayor, to Plaza de España. En route it passes the **Palacio Real** (Royal Palace) set among formal gardens on a bluff overlooking the Manzanares Valley. Philip V commissioned this imposing French-style palace on the site of the old Moorish fort, and furnished its 2,000 rooms (more than any other European palace) in a suitably regal fashion. A working palace, its opening hours are unpredictable. Check with the tourist office, and try to join one of the hour-long tours which visit around 50 rooms, including the overwhelmingly roccoco Gasparini Room, the Ceremonial Dining Room

28

Madrid Highlights

Centro de Arte Reina Sofía, Santa Isabel 52. Tel. 467 50 62. *Open*: Monday, Wednesday to Saturday 10am-9pm, Sunday 10am-2.30pm. *Admission*: 400 pta. *Metro*: Atocha. Major modern art museum. (See p.31).

Convento de las Descalzas Reales, Plaza de las Descalzas. Tel. 521 27 79. *Open*: Tuesday, Thursday, Saturday 10.30am-12.30pm and 4pm-5.30pm. *Admission*: 600 pta. *Metro*: Callao. The 16th-century Convent of the Barefoot Royals has been handsomely endowed with art treasures. (See p.30).

Museo Arqueológico, Calle Serrano 13. Tel. 577 79 12. *Open*: Tuesday to Sunday 9.15am-1.45pm. *Admission*: 400 pta. *Metro*: Serrano. An overview of Spain's cultural heritage illustrated by archaeological finds. Also a fascinating replica of the Altamira cave complex in the gardens.

Museo del Prado, Paseo del Prado. Tel. 429 28 36. *Open*: Tuesday to Saturday 9am-7pm, Sunday 9am-2pm. *Admission*: 400 pta. One of Europe's most famous art museums – not to be missed. Housed in 18th-century neo-classical grandeur, the museum displays art treasures amassed by the Spanish monarchy. (See p.30).

Fundación Thyssen-Bornemisza, Paseo del Prado 8. *Open*: Tuesday to Sunday 10am-7pm. *Admission*: 600 pta. *Metro*: Banco. Some 800 superb artworks on semi-permanent loan. (See p.31).

Palacio Real, Calle de Bailén. Tel. 542 00 59. *Open*: Monday to Saturday 10am-1.30pm and 4pm-6.15pm, Sunday 10am-1.30pm in summer; Monday to Saturday 10am-12.45pm and 3.30pm-5.15pm, Sunday 10am-12.45pm in winter (closed on state occasions). *Admission*: 800 pta. *Metro*: Opera. Principal royal residence of the Spanish kings from Philip V in the mid-18th century until Alfonso XIII went into exile in 1931. (See p.28).

Real Academia de Bellas Artes, Alcalá 13. Tel. 522 14 91. *Open*: Tuesday to Saturday 9am-7pm, Sunday and Monday 9am-2pm. *Admission*: 200 pta. *Metro*: Sol. Undervisited, with none of the Prado bustle and crowds, this is a good place to take time over the Goya paintings exhibited here. (See p.30).

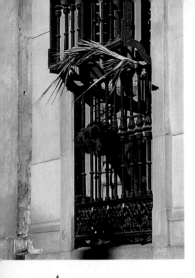

A watchdog keeps an eye on the city (above); Goya's Maja Desnuda in the Prado (right).

with seating for 145 guests, and the Throne Room with its stunning Tiepolo ceiling frescoes. Other diversions to see include the Royal Armoury, Pharmacy and Library (additional entry charges).

Lined with shops, hotels, restaurants, theatres, cafés and nightclubs, the main thoroughfare of Madrid, **Gran Vía**, cuts a broad path west-east from Plaza de España to the traffic maelstrom around Plaza de la Cibeles, so named for the Cybele Fountain which has a sculpture of a Greek fertility goddess. Midway along Gran Vía, at Plaza del Callao, there are two excellent pedestrianized shopping streets in Calle de Preciados and Calle del Carmen. Art lovers should also stop off here to inspect the treasures housed in the 16th-century **Convento de las Descalzas Reales**.

Back at the Puerta del Sol, head east along Calle de Alcalá for the **Museo de la Academia Real de Bellas Artes** (Museum of the Royal Academy), which boasts a fine collection of paintings by Goya among others; or head for the fabulous **Museo del Prado**, to the southeast via Carrera de S. Jerónimo.

The Prado houses what is indisputably the world's greatest collection of Spanish paintings, and a particularly strong set of Italian and Flemish masterpieces. If time is short, plan ahead and decide what you want to see beforehand. A likely top-of-the-list to see are works by El Greco (1541-1614), Ribera (*c.*1591-1652), Zurbarán (1598-1664), Philip IV's court painter Velázquez (1599-1660) whose *Las Meninas* (Maids of Honour) is said to be Spain's favourite painting, Murillo (1617-82), and the magnificent Goya (1746-1828). Of the Dutch and Flemish works, be sure not to miss Hieronymous Bosch, called El Bosco here, and Rubens. The Italian Old Masters include Raphael, Titian and Tintoretto.

Nearby, a Prado annexe, the **Casón del Buen Retiro**, houses the museum's treasure trove of 19th-century Spanish art, while opposite the main museum, the **Fundación Thyssen-Bornemisza** spans 700 years of artistic endeavour from the Italian primitives to Pop Art. The latter forms part of Madrid's 'Golden Triangle of Art' with the Prado, and the **Centro de Arte Reina Sofía**, which boasts important collections of modern art and Picasso's monumental *Guernica*, which was inspired by the

horrific Civil War bombing of a Basque village.

If the sightseeing and the bustle get too much, the enormous city centre **Parque del Retiro** behind the Prado is a favourite spot for *madrileños* out for a stroll. Originally a 17th-century Habsburg hunting ground, it offers 121ha (300 acres) of leafy avenues, flower beds, park benches, a rose garden, boating lake and Sunday morning sideshows.

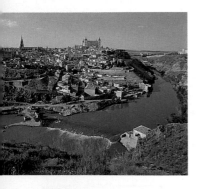

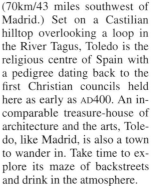

*E*l Greco's adopted home town, Toledo crowns a strategic **32** hilltop ringed by the Tagus river.

There are also cafés, exhibitions in the Palacio de Cristal and Palacio de Velázquez, plus a botanical garden founded by Carlos III in 1781.

AROUND MADRID

Toledo

(70km/43 miles southwest of Madrid.) Set on a Castilian hilltop overlooking a loop in the River Tagus, Toledo is the religious centre of Spain with a pedigree dating back to the first Christian councils held here as early as AD400. An incomparable treasure-house of architecture and the arts, Toledo, like Madrid, is also a town to wander in. Take time to explore its maze of backstreets and drink in the atmosphere.

When the city was recaptured from the Moors in 1085, many mosques were turned into churches. Then, in 1222, work began on the magnificent Gothic **Catedral**, hemmed in by a clutter of back streets. The basilica's **coro** (choir) and main altar are marvels of

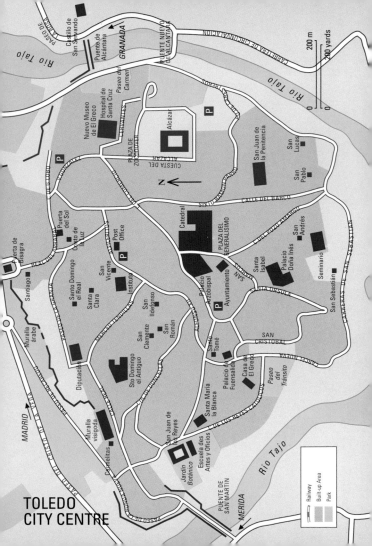

**TOLEDO
CITY CENTRE**

Toledo Steel

Toledo is famous all over the world for the quality of its steel, and swords have been forged here since Roman times. According to legend, the special property of the steel is inherited from the magical water of the River Tagus. Look out for damascene steel souvenirs. This is a craft unique to the city, which involves inlaying black steel with decorative gold, copper and silver filigree.

woodcarving. Just behind the main chapel, Narciso Tomé's baroque **Transparente** is an 18th-century masterpiece. In the **Sala Capitular** (Chapter House) there is an intricate ceiling in the Mudéjar style. Don't miss the **Tesoro** (Treasury), or the **Sacristy** with its religious artworks, including 16 paintings by El Greco.

The **Alcázar**, a fortress destroyed and rebuilt many times since the Roman era, now houses an Army Museum and has displays relating to a 72-day Civil War siege. Just to the

*F*lamboyant carvings at the monastery-church of San Juan de los Reyes, Toledo.

north, the main square, **Plaza de Zocodover**, derives its name from the Moorish market (*zoco*) held here in the Middle Ages. Beyond the horseshoe-shaped arch, in Calle de Cervantes, the 16th-century **Hospital de Santa Cruz** (Holy Cross Hospital) now houses a museum which displays a wide selection of El Greco's works.

West of the cathedral and topped by its landmark Mudéjar tower, the church of **Santo Tomé** exhibits El Greco's *Burial of the Count of Orgaz*. A magical fusion of the mundane and the spiritual, it depicts local noblemen at the count's funeral, which was attended, according to tradition, by St Augustine and St Stephen. **35**

El Greco spent the most productive years of his prolific painting career in Toledo. Just downhill from Santo Tomé, a house in which he is said to have lived has been reconstructed and linked to a museum. The **El Greco House** was originally built by Samuel Levi, a 14th-century Jewish financier and friend of King Peter I of Castile. As devout as he was rich, Levi built a synagogue next to his home, **La Sinagoga del Tránsito**. Muslim artists adorned the walls with intricate filigrees and inscriptions in Hebrew from the Psalms. Today, it's a national monument. Attached to the synagogue is a **Museum of Spanish Judaism**.

Finally, a Toledo church with regal connections: Ferdinand and Isabella built **San Juan de los Reyes** (St John of the Kings) in a mix of Mudéjar, Gothic and Renaissance styles. On the façade, look out for the chains once used by the Moors to secure their Christian prisoners. There is also a superb double-layer cloister with **36** elaborate stone carvings.

Ávila

(112km/70 miles northwest of Madrid.) If you are visiting Madrid in summer, you will appreciate the cool, refreshing mountain air of Ávila, situated 1,128m (3,700ft) above sea level. Nominated as a national monument in its entirety, the town is encircled by 2km (1.5 miles) of fairytale 11th-century battlements punctuated by 88 towers and no less than 2,500 niches suitable for sentries or marksmen.

Forming part of the eastern defences, the 12th- to 16th-century **cathedral** combines Romanesque, Gothic and Renaissance elements. Just outside the city walls, the **Basilica de San Vicente**, commemorating St Vincent of Zaragoza and his two sisters martyred in the 4th century, is noted for an extraordinary tomb topped by a bizarre oriental canopy.

A melancholy history surrounds the royal **Monasterio de Santo Tomás**, sponsored by Ferdinand and Isabella. Their only son, Don Juan, died here at the age of 19. His two

Church dignitaries parade their finest vestments for the Feast of Sta Teresa of Ávila.

tutors are buried in a small chapel near the tomb of the prince. This monastery was also the headquarters of the highly notorious Torquemada, Spain's first Grand Inquisitor.

Many visitors stop in Ávila to honour Sta Teresa of Jesus. Teresa de Cepeda y Ahumada was born in Ávila in 1515, and the convent of **Santa Teresa** marks the site of her birthplace. The frail but tireless reformer spent 30 years in the Convent of the Incarnación (outside the city walls) as a novice and later as prioress.

After you have seen Ávila up close, drive or take a bus across the Río Adaja to the monument called **Los Cuatro Postes** (The Four Posts). This rocky hill offers a panoramic view of the whole of medieval Ávila. At sunset, this walled city, wrapped in a time warp, looks almost unreal. **37**

El Escorial

(49km/30 miles northwest of Madrid.) Sheer statistics cannot do justice to the extravagant scale of this 16th-century royal palace complex. El Escorial comprises living quarters, a church, monastery, mausoleum and museum all under one roof. In a distinctly Spanish version of the Italian Renaissance style, this massive edifice boasts 86 stairways, more than 1,200 doors and 2,600 windows, and sums up the physical and spiritual superlatives of the empire's Golden Age.

Of the dozens of works of art collected in the great **basilica**, none attracts more admiration than Cellini's life-sized marble crucifix. Philip II, who ordered El Escorial to be built, died here in 1598. He is buried in the royal **pantheon**, together with the remains of almost all Spain's monarchs and their families from the 17th century onwards.

Above ground again, the **library** contains some 40,000 rare books plus priceless and beautiful manuscripts. From here, tours progress on to the **Palacio Real** (Royal Palace), and a succession of lavishly decorated rooms, notably the **Sala de las Batallas**, adorned with frescoes depicting complex battle scenes. The tapestries are also a highlight.

The **apartments of Philip II** are modest in comfort but rich in art work, and include a fantastic triptych by Hieronymus Bosch. In addition to the treasures of El Escorial, the **New Museums** display masterpieces by Ribera, Tintoretto, Velázquez and El Greco.

Segovia

(88km/55 miles northwest of Madrid.) A vision of medieval Spain with a fairytale castle at its heart, Segovia juts out from a high plateau adrift in the rolling Castilian landscape.

Marching through the centre of town, Segovia's **Roman aqueduct** is both a work of art and a triumph of engineering. This granite aqueduct is nearly 1km (half a mile) long and up to 30m (99ft) high, it has been

transporting water to the town for over 100 generations.

Founded in the 12th century, Segovia's royal castle, the **Alcázar**, was the venue for Philip II's marriage to Anne of Austria in 1570. In truth, the castle's romantic superstructure dates from the late 19th century, when it was restored after a fire.

Begun in 1525, and topped by a plethora of pinnacles and cupolas, the **cathedral** was the last of the great Spanish Gothic churches. Fine stained-glass windows illuminate the interior. Other attractions around town include the 12th-century

Gothic grace: Segovia Cathedral, completed in 1590, dominates the Plaza Mayor.

church of **San Martin**, a Romanesque beauty on Segovia's most charming square. Just outside the 11th-century city walls, stretching for 3km (1½ miles) the 12-sided church of **Vera Cruz** dates from the 13th century. Perhaps the best of the town's many fine ancient chapels, this is where the Knights of the Holy Sepulchre held court in the circular nave. **39**

Barcelona

Spain's second largest city, Barcelona is the capital of semi-autonomous Catalonia, a dynamic and strongly independent region with its own language, history, traditions and folklore. Industrious Catalans can take or leave *siesta* and dance the stately *sardaña* rather than engage in the histrionics of flamenco – but they do have a passion for all things Catalan, including their language which is almost always spoken in preference to Castilian. Catalans also like to live well, so you will find plenty of good shopping, fine restaurants and a pulsating after-dark scene in Barcelona's *bars modernos* – some of Europe's hottest nightspots.

Barcelona flourished in the 12th-14th centuries when the superb medieval old town, the Barri Gòtic (Gothic Quarter), was founded. Industrialization provided a further economic and cultural boost in the late 19th century, which also saw the Moderniste architect Antoni Gaudí adorn the city with his fantastic creations. Franco's repressive regime aimed to suppress traditional Catalan culture and language. Since his death, however, Barcelona and the region as a whole has undergone a form of renaissance – a process crowned by the hosting of the Olympic Games in 1992.

Barcelona's many attractions are widely spread around the city. The **Bus Turistic** (mid-June to September) provides a handy hop-on, hop-off

service around the main sights, and includes free cable car, funicular and tram rides for Montjuïc and Tibidabo, plus reduced admission to several sights. Details are available from any tourist office. There is also an excellent *metro* (subway) system, which operates daily from 6am to 11pm.

The city's main downtown thoroughfare, **La Rambla**, is more than just a street – it's an event. Part-traffic jam, part-promenade, part-flower market, it links the city centre Plaça de Catalunya with the harbour. It also divides the historic delights, tempting shops and friendly tapas bars and restaurants of the Barri Gòtic from the rundown and distinctly less appealing Barri Xines. Midway down La Rambla, the

Artworks in Plaça del Pi (left); and aerial views of the Barcelona waterfront (below).

Where to Go

**W**eird and wonderful: a mosaic lizard in Antoni Gaudí's fantastic Parc Güell.

19th-century covered market, **La Boqueria**, is a city highlight with mounds of glossy fruit and vegetables, seafood, sausages, meat, poultry, herbs, spices and sweetmeats.

A short step away, heading for the harbour, the famous **Liceu** opera house is a local institution. A little further on, Gaudí's fortress-like **Palau Güell**, on Nou de la Rambla, was built for his major sponsor in 1885. Across the main street, a passage leads into the café-filled arcades of the fine

Plaça Reial; and down by the harbour, the **Monument a Colom** honouring Christopher Columbus, is not far from the **Museu Marítimo**, tracing 700 years of maritime history.

The narrow alleyways and historic buildings of the **Barri Gòtic** cluster around the imposing **Catedral**. Founded in the 13th century, its 19th-century façade overlooks sudden outbreaks of the *sardaña* on summer weekends, and there is a graceful garden cloister. Nearby, there are two fascinating museums in the **Museu d'Història de la Ciutat** (City History Museum) and the **Museu Frederic Marès**, with its eclectic miscellany of religious objects and art from around the world.

Among the galleries on Carrer de Montcada, the **Museu Picasso** is the city's most popular museum, and is a short walk from the pure, Gothic beauty of **Santa María del Mar** church, near the waterfront. To the east, the spacious, green expanse of the **Parc Ciutadella** – its name derives from an 18th-century French

Barcelona Highlights

Monastir de Pedralbes, Baixada del Monestir 9. Tel. 203 92 82. *Open*: Tuesday to Sunday 10am-2pm (Saturday until 5pm). *Admission*: 300 pta. for church and cloister, 300 pta. for Thyssen-Bornemisza collection. *Metro*: Palau Reial (15-min. walk); or bus 22. Catalan Gothic architecture; Old Master paintings. (See p.44).

Museu d'Història de la Ciutat (City History Museum), Plaça del Rei. Tel. 315 11 11. *Open*: Tuesday to Saturday 10am-2pm and 4pm-8pm, Sunday 10am-2pm. *Admission*: 300 pta. *Metro*: Jaume I. An archaeological dig delves into the city's Roman origins; and the joint ticket includes the Throne Room of the Palau Reial (Royal Palace). (See p.42).

Museu Marítimo, Porta de la Pau 1. Tel. 318 32 45. *Open*: Tuesday to Saturday 9.30am-1pm and 4pm-7pm, Sunday 10am-2pm. 300 pta. Fascinating maritime museum laid out in the 14th-century royal dockyards. (See p.42).

Museu Nacional d'Art de Catalunya, Palau Nacional, Montjuïc. Tel. 423 71 99. Closed for refurbishment; check with tourist office for details. Catalonia's impressive national art collection features entire Catalan church interiors and notable Spanish art from the 16th-18th centuries. (See p.44).

Museu Picasso, Carrer de Montcada 15-19. Tel. 319 63 10. *Open*: Tuesday to Saturday 10am-8pm, Sunday 10am-3pm. 500 pta. Childhood dabbles, plus many paintings, drawings and ceramics donated by family and friends. (See p.42).

Poble Espanyol, Montjuïc. Tel. 325 78 66. *Open*: Monday 9am-8pm, Tuesday to Thursday 9am-2am, Friday and Saturday 9am-4am, Sunday 9am-midnight. *Admission*: 650 pta, family ticket 1,300 pta. Spain in miniature with traditional bars, restaurants and entertainment. (See p.44).

Sagrada Família, Plaça Sagrada Família. Tel. 455 02 47. *Open*: daily 9am-8pm. *Admission*: 700 pta. *Metro*: Sagrada Família. Gaudí's mind-boggling unfinished cathedral. For more about Gaudí, pick up a free copy of the Gaudí brochure at the tourist office (free). (See p.44).

prison torn down with much glee in 1869 – encompasses paths, gardens and ponds, an elaborate Gaudí fountain and one of Europe's better zoos.

Barcelona's historic Jewish community once lived on the slopes of **Montjuïc** (Hill of the Jews), which looms up behind the harbour crowned by the 17th-century **Castillo de Montjuïc**. The castle offers spectacular views of the city and also houses a military museum. Other attractions clinging to the city's steep hillsides include the **Parc Atraccions Montjuïc** fun fair; witty abstract art in the form of the **Fundació Joan Miró**; a brace of state-of-the-art Olympic arenas; and the **Poble Espanyol** (Spanish Village), which showcases Spanish architecture and traditions with miniature replicas of palaces, castles and churches, plus artisans' workshops, concerts and evening flamenco performances. Art lovers should not miss the world-class collections of Romanesque and Gothic art displayed in the **Museu Nacional d'Art de Catalunya** (Catalan

Art Museum). Nearby is the **Plaça Carlos Buigas**, the centrepiece of spectacular weekend light shows held from April to September.

To get to grips with Gaudí's unique architectural style, the surrealistic **Sagrada Família** (Holy Family) church is a must. An unfinished masterpiece started in 1882 (and still in progress), its 100m (330ft) towers are local landmarks. Other Gaudían highlights include tours of the **Casa Milà** rooftops at Passeig de Gràcia 92; the façade of **Casa Battló**, down the street at no. 43; and the fascinating, weird and wonderful **Parc Güell**.

On the western edge of the city, the beautiful **Monastir de Pedralbes** deserves a special mention. It was founded by Queen Elisenda in 1326, and has a charming cloister and an exceptional selection of paintings on loan from the Thyssen-Bornemisza art collection. And then last, but by no means least, the popular amusement park at **Tibidabo** combines the best in old and new technology rides, offering

BARCELONA CITY CENTRE

GERONA

GERONA

500 m

500 yards

Sagrada Familia

C. DE LOS ALMOGAVERS

Esta. del Norte

Museu d'Art Modern

Parc Zoològic

AV DE SANTA MARIA D'ARET

C DE GEN

PAS DE SANT JOAN

PDE SANT JOAN

Somorrostro

Museu Picasso

Estació França

Barri Gòtic

Catedral

Pal de la Virreina

Universitat

Museu Marítim

Cable Car

Estació Morrot Municipal

Fundació Joan Miró

Palau Nacional

Feria de Muestras

Estadi Olímpic

Funicular

Museu Militar

Castell de Montjuïc

Montjuïc

Poble Espanyol

Estació Sants

AIRPORT

N

GRAN VIA DE LES CORTS CATALANES

Railway
Built-up Area
Park

spectacular views from its perfect perch on a 542m (1,778ft) peak in the western hills overlooking Barcelona.

If you want to hit the beach in summer, it is preferable to head out of the city either north to the cliffs and coves of the Costa Brava, or south to the sweeping sandy beaches of the Costa Dorada (see p.101). However, there are half-a-dozen beaches and some *balneario* (public swimming pools) fronting **Barceloneta** (a good spot for fish restaurants), north of the harbour.

AROUND BARCELONA

Montserrat

(40km/25 miles northwest of Barcelona.) For 700 years, pilgrims have been climbing the mighty rock formation to the monastery of Montserrat, the spiritual home of Catalonia and one of Spain's most important pilgrim sites. There have been hermitages here since medieval times, possibly built to escape Moorish invasion. In 880, the Benedictines founded a monastery on this

site, 1,135m (3,725ft) above the Llobregat river valley.

During the 12th century, Montserrat became the repository of *La Moreneta*, a Black Madonna statue said to have been made by St Luke and brought to Barcelona by St Peter, and pilgrims have come to worship here ever since.

In 1808, Napoleon's troops destroyed the original monastery, so the present building dates from 1874. Montserrat is still very much an active monastery, and visitors may only enter the beautiful Gothic cloister, the basilica and the museum. A highlight of any visit is a recital by the famous **Escalonia Boys' Choir** (daily 12.45pm), while the **museum** features artworks by El Greco, Picasso and modern Catalan artists, as well as interesting archaeological treasures.

Sadly, rampant commercialization has invaded Montserrat's grounds. However, it is easy to escape the crowds on one of the four well-signposted walks to former hermitages and the Santa Cova (the Holy Cave, where La Moreneta was

*C*atalans prefer the stately sardaña (left); Montserrat's pilgrim monastery (above).

allegedly discovered) in the magnificent protected mountain parkland.

Poblet

(133km/83 miles west of Barcelona.) Once you have seen one monastery, you have definitely not seen them all. The medieval monastery and fortress of Poblet contrasts sharply with Montserrat.

47

For a start, few tourists crowd Poblet, though it is the largest and best preserved Cistercian monastery in Europe. Founded in 1151 by the Count of Barcelona, Ramon Berenguer, as a gesture of thanksgiving for the Reconquest of

The Pont del Diable once transported water from Riu Gayo to Roman Tarraconensis.

Catalonia, it sprawls upon a plateau amid fertile hills. Loyal royal patronage ensured fame, fortune and historical importance for the monastery. At one time around 200 monks lived and worked here. Today there are just 30.

As you enter the grounds, Poblet's façade is a majestic sight. A guided tour leads past the wine cellars, library, chapter house and refectory into the Romanesque and Gothic-style church and spacious cloister with its rose garden.

Tarragona

(95km/60 miles south of Barcelona.) The Romans came ashore at Tarragona in the 3rd century BC, and rapidly established it as an important military and political headquarters. *Tarraco*, as it was then known, quickly grew to a population of 30,000, minted its own currency and by 27BC was the capital of Hispania Citerior, the largest Roman province on the Iberian peninsula. Local archaeological finds and monuments – some of the finest to

Andorra: Shangri-La in the Pyrenees

The tiny (487sq km/188sq mile) principality of Andorra is the world's only country whose official language is Catalan. After seven centuries of fiercely defended independence, it is now a cosmopolitan tax haven regularly invaded by coachloads of bargain hunters on a mission to plunder the bulging shops of Carrer Meritxell in Andorra-la-Vella, the capital. It is a shame that the principality's spectacular scenery takes second place to the shopping frenzy, for its verdant valleys backed by rugged mountains, country villages and fine old Romanesque churches are a delight. Andorra also has well-equipped winter sports resorts.

have survived from this period – include the city walls, the amphitheatre, a great aqueduct, and the contents of several good museums.

Tarragona's most impressive Roman monument is the 1st-century **Pont del Diable** some 4km (2.5 miles) north of the town centre, off the N240 towards Lleida (Lérida). The 'Devil's Bridge' is actually a perfectly preserved two-storey aqueduct, which spans 217m (712ft) and rises to a height of 27m (88ft) above ground.

The Rambla Vella (Old Rambla) neatly divides Tarragona in half. To the north is

the old walled city; to the south is the Rambla Nova (New Rambla) and the newer part of town. Take a walk along the **Passeig Arqueològic** which follows the top of the old city walls enclosing a labyrinthine maze of charming medieval streets.

In this atmospheric corner of town, the **Museu Arqueològic**, Plaça del Rei, hosts a modern, well-designed exhibition of delicate mosaics and other ancient artefacts. Next door, the **Pretori Romà** (Roman Praetorium), is thought to have been part of the original complex belonging to the **49** provincial administration. It was restored in the Middle Ages and today houses the atmospheric **Museu d'Història** (History Museum).

Walking from here towards the sea brings you to the ruins of the Roman **amphitheatre**, built into the hillside. Gladiators fought here, and the first martyrdom of Christians in Spain took place at this site in AD259. Tarragona's most important ancient site beyond the city walls, the **Necròpoli i Museu Paleocristià** (Necropolis and Paleo-Christian Museum), stands at the place of the city's early Christian burial-ground. Excavations have uncovered over 2,000 graves, and you will find the best archeological discoveries displayed in the museum.

Medieval Tarragona's pride and joy is its great **cathedral**, the largest in Catalonia, founded in 1171. The 12th- to 13th-century cloister is an attraction in its own right; and the **Museu Diocesà** harbours a fine collection of art treasures and Flemish tapestries. The antique cobbled streets around

the cathedral exude an air of picturesque decay. Here you'll find the **Casa Museu Castellarnau**, an 18th to 19th-century mansion with sumptuous period fittings, which has recently been renovated.

Back in the modern part of town, the **Balco del Mediterrani** looks down onto Tarragona's commercial port, one of the busiest in the Mediterranean. The adjacent fishing port is worthy of a visit for its fish restaurants.

Vilafranca del Penedès

(54km/34 miles southwest of Barcelona.) Situated on a fertile plain half-way between Barcelona and Tarragona, Vilafranca lies at the heart of one of Spain's best-known wine regions. There are no *bodegas* to visit in the centre of town, but the tourist office can supply a list of welcoming vineyards nearby.

You will find however, the **Museu dei Vi** (wine museum), housed in a medieval palace once owned by the counts of Barcelona and the kings of

Aragon. Dioramas illustrate the story of wine through the ages. The wine museum shares its quarters with the **Museu Municipal** which is devoted to archeology, natural history and Catalan religious art. From the third-floor windows, you may see a monument to another of the town's passions – a human pyramid of *castellers*. A type of Catalan folk troupe comprised of men and boys, the *castellers* climb barefoot on each other's shoulders to form precarious human towers up to seven storeys high.

Vilafranca's leafy *rambla* and old town centre are full of character, particularly on a Saturday when they host one of the region's most colourful, general **markets**. Also visit the splendid basilica of **Santa María**, the adjacent Palais Baltà, and the church of **Sant Francesc**, famous for its Catalan Gothic treasures.

Grape harvesting at the Torres vineyard, a market leader in the Penedès region.

Central Spain – Land of El Cid and Don Quixote

Central Spain is home to the most soul-stirring and archetypal Spanish landscape. The great, windswept plains of the Castilian *meseta* (plateau), the wine country of La Rioja, and atmospheric La Mancha – Don Quixote's stamping ground – are dotted with isolated castles and ancient windmills. Here, vast spaces open up with a scale and grandeur unrivalled in Europe.

SALAMANCA

Dating from Iberian times, Salamanca is one of the greatest cities of Spain. During the Roman era the city walls were constructed and a bridge (still standing) was built across the Río Tormes. Later, Moorish

*P*icturesque Cuenca, famous for its medieval clifftop Casas Colgadas (hanging houses).

and Christian forces fought on and off over the city, until, in 1178, Ferdinand II of León assembled his parliament here, ensuring Salamanca's future importance and prosperity.

At the heart of the town, the **Plaza Mayor** (Main Square) built in the 18th century is considered to be the most perfect plaza in Spain. To the south, Salamanca's two cathedrals, which throw up a thicket of spiky spires and turrets, are contiguous; you enter the old through the new. Construction of the **Catedral Nueva** began in 1513. Inside, the triple-naved cathedral has marvellous baroque choir stalls and 18 side chapels, most notably the **Capilla Dorada** (Golden Chapel) with 110 sculptures.

After the grandeur of the New Cathedral, the **Catedral Vieja**, seems as intimate as a private chapel. Highlights of this Romanesque building include the 15th-century main altar; a retable featuring a fine 12th-century statue known as the Virgen de la Vega; and the unusual Mudéjar dome in the **Capilla de Talavera**. The **53**

Diocesan Museum in the old chapter house has a notable collection of paintings by Fernando Gallego, an underrated master of 15th-century Hispano-Flemish style.

The **Universidad** (University) of Salamanca, founded in 1218, was one of the greatest centres of learning in medieval Europe. The main building's 16th-century plateresque façade is unbelievably intricate and the lecture halls around the central patio illustrate centuries of architectural and decorative detail. Nearby, the **Patio de las Escuelas** is surrounded by plateresque buildings. Make sure you don't miss the terrific 15th-century **Casa de las Conchas** (House of Shells), just south of Plaza Mayor; its exterior walls are studded with hundreds of scallop shell motifs.

SALAMANCA TO LEÓN

A strategic walled stronghold above the right bank of the Río Duero, the often besieged city of **Zamora** changed hands many times in the centuries of

The cathedral in Astorga, a small pilgrim town between León and Salamanca.

the Reconquest. For the best view of this appealing historic city, cross the Duero by the 14th-century bridge. From the south bank, you can admire the Byzantine cupola of the **cathedral**, built in the 12th century and roofed in curved stone tiles laid like fish scales. Its interior features a notable retable by Fernando Gallego, and there is a tapestry museum in the cloister.

East of Zamora, the medieval hilltop town of **Toro** is a national monument. Besides some splendid Romanesque churches, convents and mansions, and a ruined 10th-century castle, Toro's greatest pride is the **Iglesia Colegiata de Santa María la Mayor** (Collegiate Church of St Mary the Great). A Romanesque classic, it houses a most unusual 16th-century painting entitled *The Virgin and the Fly*, which is

widely considered to be the best-known likeness of Isabella of Castile.

LEÓN

León is a prosperous, modern city, with a welcoming ancient heart. It does not receive too many tourists, but those who do make the effort to visit are amply rewarded.

The most magnificent monument in the town is the 13th-century **Catedral de Santa María de Regla**. Clearly inspired by the French Gothic cathedral at Chartres, it has the most glorious complement of stained glass in all Spain – 125 huge windows and 57 smaller glassed areas dating from the 13th-20th centuries. The west façade sports mismatched towers and elaborately carved portals. Tours of the cloister, an elegant mix of Gothic and Renaissance elements, lead to the **Diocesan Museum**, which exhibits archeological finds, fine and applied arts.

A few streets west of the cathedral, an equestrian statue of St Isidore crowns the south side of the **Colegiata de San Isidoro** (Collegiate Church). In the Moorish invasions, the saint's relics were evacuated to **55**

León from Seville, where he had been archbishop, and still attract pilgrims to this day. Next door, the naïve frescoes in the **Panteón Real** (Royal Pantheon), burial place of several kings and princes, are so wonderful it has been dubbed 'the Sistine Chapel of Romanesque Art'.

The former **Monasterio de San Marco** rejoices in a formidable plateresque façade. Intended as a hospice for the medieval pilgrims, Ferdinand the Catholic spared no expense in turning it into a showpiece for the Knights of St James, and today it is one of Spain's finest *paradores* (see p.175). Non-residents are welcome to explore. The cloister and sacristy of the monastery house the **Museo Arqueológico Provincial**. Its collections run the gamut from Roman mosaics to Romanesque sculpture.

VALLADOLID

The biggest and most industrialized city of this region, Valladolid may lack the historical charm of León, yet there is much here for students of architecture and sculpture, and there are also glimpses of Cervantes and Columbus. Valladolid is one of the hotbeds of the Isabelline style – a form of overblown plateresque expressed in extravagant, florid

*A*fter writing Don Quixote, Cervantes occupied this quiet townhouse on Calle del Rastro.

ornamentation. It is named after Isabella of Castile, whose fateful marriage to Ferdinand of Aragon took place in Valladolid in 1469.

Visitors plunge right into the mainstream of Isabelline decoration at the **Colegio de San Gregorio**, proud possessor of an unusually elaborate façade. The college houses the **Museo Nacional de Escultura** (National Museum of Sculpture), the 'Prado' of religious statuary with works ranging from the 13th to the 18th centuries. The star here is the woodcarving genius of the Spanish Renaissance, Alonso Berruguete, said to have studied under Michelangelo. His martyrs seem to shed real tears and blood.

Another talent on show is Juan de Juni, an Italian-trained Frenchman of the mid-16th century. Juni's altarpiece in the **cathedral** is the highlight of a rich display of art, contained within walls designed by Juan de Herrera, co-creator of Philip II's Escorial complex.

Some famous names are linked with the city, including Philip II and Philip IV, who were both born here. In 1506, Christopher Columbus died in the arcaded two-storey **Casa-Museo de Colón** (House-Museum of Columbus), now restored to display relics and documents relating to the Age of Discovery. The **Casa de Cervantes** commemorates author Miguel Cervantes, creator of *Don Quixote*, who lived for several years in this ivy-covered house.

AROUND VALLADOLID

Coca Castle lies 63km (39 miles) south of Valladolid. In Castile it is only natural to expect to see castles, but few if any are finer than this masterpiece of Spanish Mudéjar military architecture in the small town of Coca. Constructed in the late 15th century for the Archbishop of Seville, Alonso de Fonseca, it has three layers of walls surrounding an impenetrable keep, and there are towers and clusters of battlements at all levels. Although it is now a forestry school, it is still open to the public.

57

From afar, **Peñafiel Castle** (35km/22 miles east of Valladolid) looks like an improbable shipwreck. It's over 200m (220yd) long, but less than 25m (28yd) across, and sits stranded high on a lonely hilltop. The formidable stronghold has a double set of ramparts and 30 towers and turrets – enough to make any enemy think again. According to legend, when King Sancho reclaimed it from the Moors in the 11th century, he is said to have announced that 'Henceforth this shall be the faithful rock (*peñafiel*) of Castile'. In the village below, the big, open sandy plaza is used for bullfights in August.

BURGOS

The one-time capital of the kingdom of Castile, Burgos is a beauty. One of the most significant resting places on the Pilgrim Way, it is still an excellent spot to stop today. The best approach is from the south, crossing the lazy Río Arlanzón to the most flamboyant of the old city gates, the **58**

Arco de Santa María. Along the river here, promenades and flower gardens follow the path of the original city wall, and it is a favourite spot for the evening *paseo* (stroll).

The great **cathedral** of Burgos, the third-biggest cathedral in Spain (after Seville and Toledo), was begun in 1221. Bristling with lacy spires, its treasures are many and varied, from Gil de Siloé's altar of St Anne, to his son Diego's exquisite golden stairway inside the Coronería portal. Don't miss the splendid **Constable's chapel**, burial place of Hernández de Velasco, Constable of Castile during the reign of the Catholic Monarchs. The local hero and legendary 11th-century warrior, El Cid, is buried beside his wife beneath the cathedral's dome.

Burgos is a wonderful city to amble through. There are busy shopping streets, inviting squares and parks, and distinguished medieval houses. Outstanding amongst the latter is the **Casa Cordón**, Plaza de Calvo Sotelo, where Ferdinand and Isabella welcomed

Columbus back from his second voyage to the New World. To the south, there's a stirring equestrian statue of El Cid before the San Pablo bridge; and, across the river, another noble Renaissance house, the Casa Miranda, serves as the **municipal museum**.

On the western outskirts of Burgos, the **Convento de las Huelgas** was founded in the 12th century. Behind fortress-like walls, the complex is something of an architectural hybrid with Romanesque elements and a superb Mudéjar-

Gothic cloister. Kings were crowned and buried here, and a small museum displays some of the ecclesiastical treasures and artworks amassed by the convent's powerful abbesses.

A few miles east of Burgos, in a forest park, is the 15th-century Carthusian monastery of **Cartuja de Miraflores** founded by Juan II. It features

The tombs of Hernández de Velasco and his wife inside the Constable's chapel.

the alabaster sepulchre of Juan and his second wife Isabella of Portugal, which is housed in the white granite church. The work of master sculptor Gil de Siloé, it is considered to be one of the finest tombs in all Spain.

Logroño

The leafy main square of this spacious modern city is big enough for a fiesta, and when it's fiesta time in Logroño you can be sure of a certain amount of wine tasting, for this is the lively capital of Spain's premier wine region, La Rioja.

Among medieval pilgrim travellers, the province of La Rioja was renowned for its cheerful and attentive hospitality. Their first stop would have been **Santa María de Palacio**, dating from the 11th century and topped by a tall, graceful, pyramid-shaped tower. A few streets to the south of the church, the **cathedral**, which is considerably younger, features a generously sculpted main portal. Behind the cathedral lie the atmospheric narrow streets of the old town.

MOVING SOUTHWARDS

Soria, the smallest provincial capital of Spain, spreads along a poplar-shaded bend of the Río Duero, and is Old Castile at its most poetic. A pedestrianized street links the main square with the Alameda de Cervantes city park, where a small chapel, the **Ermita de la Soledad**, contains a treasured 16th-century wooden statue of Christ. Across the street, the **Museo Numantino** (Museum of Numancia) specializes in relics found in the Roman ruins just north of town. Numancia was a Celtiberian city.

Soria's collection of churches, in mellow toast-coloured stone, is bountiful and beautiful. All date from the 12th century, and among the most important are: **Santo Domingo**, with an expansive Romanesque façade; **San Juan de Rabanera**, with Byzantine touches and an early hint of Gothic; and the **Co-catedral de San Pedro**, with a plateresque portal and a Romanesque cloister.

All but hidden on the left bank of the river, **San Juan de Duero** used to be a monastery of the Knights Templar. The remains of the original Romanesque-Oriental **cloister** reveal finely carved capitals, and the church now serves as the medieval section of the Museo Numantino.

A sleepy town northeast of Madrid, **Sigüenza** is home to a classic fortress, an outsized (for this small town at least) cathedral and the lovely **Plaza Mayor**, one of the most beautiful main squares in Spain.

Founded by Visigoths and occupied by Moors, Sigüenza's **fort** was reconquered by Christian forces early in the 12th century. It became the headquarters of the bishops of Sigüenza, and housed around 1,000 soldiers and more than 300 horses during the 15th century. Today, it is a *parador*.

At first sight the crenellated **cathedral** also resembles a fortress. However, it contains a wealth of sculptural features, of which the most celebrated is the **sepulchre of 'El Doncel'** ('The Page'). Commissioned by Queen Isabella, it honours a young servant killed fighting in Granada in 1486. Opposite, the **Museo Diocesano de Arte** packs its 14 halls with everything from prehistoric axes to an ethereal rendering of the Virgin by Zurbarán.

Teruel, the capital of Lower Aragon, is a prime showcase for Mudéjar-style architecture. When Alfonso II of Aragon captured the town from the Moors in 1171, most Muslims chose to stay until their enforced expulsion at the end of the 15th century. This was time enough for the creation of lasting works of Mudéjar art.

The city's **cathedral** has some intriguing Mudéjar elements, especially the finely decorated 13th-century brick tower and the lantern in the dome. There are also two other local towers which are considered to be classics of this style: the **Torre San Martin** and **Torre del Salvador**.

Spanish tourists are likely to make a bee-line for the Gothic **Iglesia de San Pedro** (St Peter's Church), but not for its 13th-century Mudéjar tower. **61**

Adjoining the church is a chapel containing the mausoleum of the Lovers of Teruel, a star-crossed 13th-century couple whose tale of love lost and early death has inspired generations of Spanish writers.

Away from the main highways in the hill country of eastern Castilla La Mancha, pretty **Cuenca** is a favourite on many tourist itineraries. The old town occupies a dramatic site perched on a precipice above the rivers Huécar and Júcar. It is here that Cuenca's famous medieval **Casas Colgadas** (Hanging Houses) literally hang out over the void.

Visitors are also drawn to Cuenca's **Museo de Arte Abstracto Español**, a collection of outstanding contemporary Spanish paintings and sculptures installed in the old town. And there is the **Museo de Cuenca**, a provincial archaeological museum which occupies a 14th-century mansion near the cathedral.

Construction of the **cathedral** began right after the Reconquest to a Gothic plan with some Norman features attributed to itinerant medieval architects. Among the treasures here is a 14th-century Byzantine diptych embellished with

*S*triped with vines and dotted by olive trees, La Mancha offers more than windmills.

precious stones, said to be the only one of its kind in Spain.

Although it's a significant dot on the map, **Ciudad Real** is, in truth, a distinctly underwhelming 'Royal City'. Sightseeing focuses on the remains of the 14th-century town wall, specifically the Puerta de Toledo, a Mudéjar gate. There are also three Gothic churches, including the cathedral, noted for its choir stalls. The church of San Pedro features fine Mudéjar and Gothic portals.

If you're planning to spend a few days following the footsteps of Don Quixote, the town of **Almagro** (25km/16 miles east of Ciudad Real) is a preferable overnight stop.

Man of La Mancha

The vast, parched plain of La Mancha, with its endless horizons and shimmering mirages was the perfect setting for the adventures of author Miguel Cervantes' myopic, idealistic knight, Don Quixote, and his squire, Sancho Panza.

Cervantes was born on the very edge of La Mancha, at Alcalá de Henares in 1547. The son of an itinerant doctor, his education was minimal. Later, travels took him to Italy, and then to Algeria as a prisoner of the Turks after the Battle of Lepanto (1571).

Back in Spain, it is said he wrote the first draft of *Don Quixote* in the prison of **Argamasilla de Alba** (northwest of Almagro). It was published in 1605 to great acclaim, and has been translated into more languages than any other book except the Bible. A sequel appeared in 1615, but a year later Cervantes was dead.

The names of several of La Mancha's villages and towns appear in the text of *Don Quixote*, none more important than **El Toboso** (in Toledo province), the home of Dulcinea, the woman of Quixote's dreams. Dulcinea's house is open to the public. **63**

Green Spain

If your idea of Spain is sun-baked white villages, *costas* lined with high-rise buildings, and swirling flamenco dancers, then think again. For this is a very different country – a green, rural, Celtic land of fishermen and farmers, where the rain in Spain falls mainly, hence the verdant landscape.

GALICIA

The ancient kingdom of Galicia, in the northwestern corner of the Iberian peninsula, is rugged and isolated, its coastline characterized by narrow rocky *rías* (sea inlets) battered by the Atlantic. It was Galicia, not sunny Andalusia, that attracted Spain's (and history's) first tourists; millions of sandal-shod medieval pilgrims hiked here from all over Europe to the shrine of St James at Santiago de Compostela.

Galicia's scalloped coastline is perfect for boating, fishing and, when the sun does shine, swimming. Although the Atlantic coast south from La Coruña has the more spectacular *rías*, the northern indentations, the **Rías Altas**, are home to several unspoiled resort towns and quiet beaches.

The medieval village of **Pontedeume** is an old-fashioned resort with a long sandy beach. **Ortigueira** is noted for its fine beach and lush hills. **El Barqueiro**, a picture-postcard fishing village, has a white sand beach and **Viveiro's** monuments offer a contrast to the fishing port and resort ambience. Popular with bathers and fishermen, **Foz** has a particularly mild micro-climate.

La Coruña

Very built-up nowadays but worth a visit for its historic port and old town, La Coruña possesses Spain's oldest lighthouse, the **Torre de Hércules**, said to be the only Roman lighthouse still in operation. Now clad in an 18th-century shell, it affords splendid Atlantic vistas from the lookout 242 steps above ground.

The Spanish Armada sailed for England (and disaster)

from La Coruña's busy **port** in 1588. Behind the port, Avenida de la Marina curves east to the **old town**, dense with historic churches and monasteries. The 16th-century **Castillo de San Antón**, guarding the harbour approaches, serves as an archaeological museum.

Santiago de Compostela

The one major town of the region, and the terminus of the Pilgrim Way, Santiago is the third holiest shrine in Christendom (after Jerusalem and Rome). It is also a lively and attractive place with beautiful buildings, colourful café-filled plazas and a largely pedestrianized heart ideal for sightseeing and relaxing.

The best-known view in Santiago is of the main façade

These glassed-in balconies in La Coruña are typical of northern Spanish seaside towns.

of the **cathedral**, looming high above the plaza with baroque adornments and twin towers – all its surfaces stained with rust-coloured moss. Historically, this is supposed to be the spot where the 9th-century Asturian kings built churches

Touching the central pillar of the Door of Glory is a traditional pilgrim gesture.

over the tomb of St James (Santiago). The present largely Romanesque edifice was undertaken after the Reconquest.

Just inside the main entrance, the 800-year-old **Pórtico de la Gloria** (Door of Glory) is a marvel of Romanesque sculpture by the artist known as Master Mateo. A 13th-century polychrome statue of St James takes the spotlight on the main altar, standing above the crypt and said to contain St James' remains. Pilgrims pass behind the statue and touch its shoulders through special holes.

At right angles to the cathedral's main entrance on Plaza del Obradoiro, the **Hostal de los Reyes Católicos** has a stupendous façade. Founded by Ferdinand and Isabella in 1499 (hence the name), the former pilgrim hostel is now a luxurious *parador* (see p.177).

Wherever you wander in Santiago de Compostela, you will be in sight of a historic church or monastery. There are plenty of bars and restaurants, serving seafood fresh from the *rías*. For an added insight into

The Legend of St James

Unsubstantiated by the Bible, the legend of St James sprang up in the 9th century when a star is supposed to have directed some Galician shepherds to the Apostle's grave. The story goes that St James brought Christianity to Spain after the death of Christ. When he returned to Judaea, he was martyred by Herod, and his disciples fled with the body in a magical vessel with no sails or crew. It ferried them to the village of Padrón, and the body was buried nearby.

Its 'discovery' in the 9th century was hailed as a miracle, and there were several more to follow, including a ghostly sighting of St James on horseback slaying Moors by the thousand at the Battle of Clavijo in 844. These exploits earned him the title 'Matamoros' or Moor Slayer. It also elevated him to the position of patron saint of the Reconquest, and of Spain.

The cult of St James spread far and wide, and by the end of the 11th century, the Pilgrim Way (Camino de Santiago) was attracting pilgrims from all over Europe. A century later, two million Christians made the trek each year.

local customs, crafts and folklore, visit the **Museo do Pobo Gallego** housed in the old convent of Santo Domingo.

THE WEST COAST

The road from Santiago de Compostela to the **Rías Bajas** (Lower Estuaries) cuts through the village of **Padrón**, believed to be the spot where the vessel carrying the remains of St James arrived. Legend has it that the vessel was tied to a mooring stone which is now displayed beneath the altar of the local church.

The *rías* themselves form a jagged coastline dotted with fishing ports and small resorts such as **La Toja**, a holiday island of pines and palms opposite **O Grove**, a fishing port which has also expanded into a popular resort.

A strategic port since the Middle Ages, **Pontevedra** is one of Galicia's most charming towns with many fine old buildings, gardens and spacious squares. The city's pride and joy is the plateresque **Iglesia de Santa María la Mayor** in the old fishermen's quarter. Its sculpted **façade** is divided into compartments each telling a New Testament story.

The patron saint of Pontevedra, the Pilgrim Virgin, is commemorated in the curvaceous 18th-century **Iglesia de la Virgen de la Peregrina**. Nearby, the **Iglesia de San Francisco** was founded in the 14th century; and the **provincial museum**, housed in interconnecting historic mansions, offers departments of archaeology, art and some enlightening exhibits on the Galician seafaring way of life.

The inhabitants of **Bayona** (Baiona) were the first to learn of Columbus' landing in the New World on 1 March 1493. Today, the town is an attractive resort, largely undiscovered by the masses. This delightful fishing port is full of traditional houses and tapas bars. Set on a *ría*, it overlooks a wooded promontory where an ancient castle has been transformed

*S*hellfish city: fishing folk hard at work bringing in the harvest mussels off Pontevedra's coast.

into a *parador* with wonderful views. Bayona's beaches are small and soon get crowded in the season. A few miles out of the village lies the wide beach of Playa de América.

Set amidst beautiful countryside, the provincial capital of **Orense** is a fairly unprepossessing place. Still, it is worth visiting the historic hub and **cathedral**, built in Romanesque-Gothic style and consecrated at the end of the 12th century. Of special interest is the triple-arched **Pórtico del Paraíso** (Paradise Portal), patterned after the Door of Glory at Santiago de Compostela. Nearby, the down-to-earth, no-frills bars crammed into narrow Calle de Lepanto, give a good impression of the unaffected nature of the people of inland Galicia.

The medieval centre of **Lugo** is enclosed by almost 2km (1.5 miles) of the best-preserved **Roman walls** in Spain. Old Lugo is a pleasant place for a stroll with a big, tree-shaded main square and historic houses and churches, including a cathedral founded in 1129. The **Museo Provincial**, housed in an old palace, has a good fine arts collection, and incorporates the cloister of the convent of San Francisco.

ASTURIAS

This is a wild, rugged province known for its fiercely independent people and potent cider. They say Asturias is the true Spain because it was the only corner of the country which did not succumb to the Moors.

After the seemingly invincible Moors had overrun most of Spain in the 8th century, a band of Christian soldiers, led by local hero Pelayo, descended from the mountains and initiated the Reconquest with a small but significant victory over the Moors at the Battle of Covadonga in 722.

A modern statue of Pelayo stands in the main square of **Covadonga** and his remains are interred in the **Santa Cueva** (Holy Cave), where Pelayo saw a vision of the Virgin Mary which inspired his victory. It is a place of pilgrimage for Asturians.

69

Oviedo

The initial impression of the Asturian capital is of an ugly, industrial city. However, press on to Oviedo's compact historic centre and you will find many a fine monument, plus a host of friendly *sidrarías*, bars serving the lethal, potent local cider (*sidra*).

Oviedo's **cathedral** culminates in a flourish with a tall Flamboyant Gothic tower. Its **Cámara Santa** (Holy Chamber) shrine was built by Alfonso II to house holy relics brought from Toledo after it fell to the Moors. Behind the cathedral, the **Museo Arqueológico** is housed in a splendid old palace-convent with a gorgeous plateresque cloister.

Beyond the city centre, you will find two remarkable examples of Visigothic architecture. A short walk to the northeast, the church of **Santullano**, built in the 9th-century, is claimed to be the oldest pre-Romanesque church in Spain. On the wooded slopes 3km (2 miles) northwest of Oviedo, **Santa María del Naranco** is believed to be the reception chamber for a palace built for Ramiro I in 842. Just up the hill, part of the former palace chapel, **San Miguel de Lillo**, has beautiful Byzantine-influenced carvings.

CANTABRIA

There is plenty of variety in Cantabria, where the sea and the snow-capped heights of the Picos de Europa can both be covered in a day's excursion. As well as fishing villages, ports and miles of seafront wilderness, the coast of Cantabria also offers several popular summer resorts, such as **Castro Urdiales**, **Laredo** and **Comillas**.

Just 25km (16 miles) from the coast, behind steep green pastures coloured with wild flowers, the great wall of the Cantabrian Mountains (*Cordillera Cantábrica*) rises to a height of 2,600m (8,530ft), culminating in the spectacular **Picos de Europa**.

The N621 cuts through the dramatic **Desfiladero de la Hermida** gorge along the

River Deva to **Potes**, the main gateway to the eastern Picos. Here you can pick up maps and walking suggestions from the tourist office. Wonderful wild flowers adorn the mountains and there is good bird-watching, too. Chamois and bears also roam around here, but are rarely seen.

A perfectly preserved medieval village of golden stone houses, cobbled streets, farmyards and patrician mansions, **Santillana del Mar** has been described as 'the prettiest village in Spain' by none other

Santillana's historic façades weighed down by galleries and coats of arms.

than Jean-Paul Sartre. At the north end of the village, the **Colegiata** (Collegiate Church) is dedicated to St Juliana (Santillana is a contraction of her name), whose tomb is inside. Its 12th-century Romanesque **cloister** is a real beauty. In the **convent** at the other end of the village, the **Museo Diocesano 71**

specializes in carvings of saints and angels gathered together from outlying churches.

Discovered in 1868, 2km (1 mile) inland from Santillana, the **Altamira** cave complex contains some of the finest and most inspiring ancient works of art in Europe. They were painted very long ago – though that is not the sole reason that they are rated so highly. These paintings of bison and other beasts are an example of astonishing draughtsmanship, in which their creators used the curvature and protuberances in the rock to give added life and motion to their subjects.

The actual caves are closed to the general public, but there is a museum which contains the 30,000-year-old remains of a caveman. At **Puente Viesgo**, 29km (18 miles) out of Santander on the Logroño road, there are four caves open to visitors. The main one, **Cueva del Castillo**, features bison and curious handprints thought to be the artist's signature.

The city of **Santander** successfully combines the roles of major port and tasteful resort, though there is little of cultural or historic interest here. Two-thirds of the town was destroyed by fire in 1941. After the fire, the **cathedral** overlooking the ancient port was reconstructed to resemble the medieval original, a mixture of a fortress and a watchtower above a Romanesque crypt. The **Museo Provincial de Prehistoria** displays notable finds from excavations around the province; and the town also boasts a fine **Museo de Bellas Artes**, featuring some powerful works by Goya.

The beach suburb of **El Sardinero** with its flower gardens and numerous seafood bars contributes to the city's resort mood. Overlooking the sea from the rugged peninsula is the Victorian-style **Magdalena Palace**, built for Alfonso XIII as a summer escape, housing a host of architectural eccentricities.

All-terrain tourists tackling the snow-covered peaks of the Picos de Europa.

The Northern Border

The area from Bilbao on the Bay of Biscay (*Mar Cantábrico* in Spanish) across to the mountains of northern Aragon – including the Basque Country and the Pyrenean province of Navarre – is remarkable for its diversity. It embraces both the main point of entry from France and some of Spain's most rugged terrain.

BASQUE COUNTRY

The Spanish Basque Country (*País Vasco*) is an autonomous region with its own language and traditions, and what many gourmets consider to be the finest cuisine in Spain. The city of **Bilbao** is the capital and the industrial heartland of the Basque Country and is the most important port of Spain. Its bustling and thriving central district, broad boulevards and leafy parks compensate to some extent for the smokestacks. The **Casco Viejo** (Old Quarter), currently undergoing heavy restoration, is full of good, cheap eating and drinking places.

For tourists, and art lovers in particular, there is one sight that clamours for attention. The **Museo de Bellas Artes** (Fine Arts Museum) is one of the country's very best collections. It offers a rich survey of Spanish classics (El Greco, Goya and an honest, 'warts and all' portrait of Philip IV by Velázquez), as well as Flemish and Italian masterpieces. The museum's upper floor is devoted to Basque and international 20th-century art.

The city of **Vitoria** (Gasteiz) was founded by the Navarrese king Sancho the Wise in 1181, and it lies somewhat off the main tourist trail on the plain south of Bilbao. In 1200, the town passed into the hands of Castile and later grew rich on its wool trade.

The medieval town centre, laid out in a concentric pattern on the fortified hilltop, is home to the 14th-century **Catedral de Santa María**. Nearby, the **Museo Provincial de Arqueología**, features Iron Age and Roman relics. The prosperous

Angelic faces gather at a Corpus Christi festival with their baskets full of rose petals.

merchants built gracious Renaissance mansions and fine churches such as **San Miguel**, on **Plaza de la Virgen Blanco** (White Virgin Square) to the south. Here, the Battle of Vitoria monument commemorates the Duke of Wellington's 1813 victory, which sent José I hightailing across the border

back to France. Just east of this plaza the city's spacious main square, **Plaza de España**, is a classic 18th-century Spanish ensemble, with the town hall on the north side.

San Sebastián (Donostia), the 'Pearl of the Cantabrian Coast', lies on the magnificent **Bahía de la Concha** (Seashell Bay), a semi-circle of sandy beaches flanked by two peninsulas. Formerly a fishing and trading port, San Sebastián was elevated to the heights of favoured royal seaside resort in the mid-19th century.

75

The charming town centre has little in the way of historical monuments, but numerous *belle-époque* villas and buildings. The Miramar Palace, and sweeping beachfront promenade along **Playa de la Concha** lend an undeniable cachet to this popular family resort. It is often referred to as one of Spain's most beautiful cities.

In the lee of Monte Urgull, the colourful streets of the **Parte Vieja** (Old Quarter) radiate from the arcaded **Plaza de la Constitución**. The atmosphere still recalls something of an old-time fishing village, and the narrow streets are the focus for the early evening walkabout when locals and visitors cram the multitude of bars and restaurants.

The city's oldest church, **San Vicente**, stands here as well as **Museo San Telmo**, displaying the municipal art collections, with sections on local history and crafts. Not far from the fishing port (summer season boat trips to the **Isla de Santa Clara** in the bay), the church of **Santa María** has an ornate baroque façade. If you want to learn more about Basque seafaring, take a look around the **Palacio del Mar**, which is both an aquarium and a museum.

Navarre

Moving from west to east, the Pyrenees gain altitude, and the Basque character of the countryside and the people recede. Navarre once extended into France, but the mountains now form a natural border between France and Spain.

Pamplona (Iruña) is world-famous for its July *encierro* (running of the bulls), and is also recommended on the non-festive days. Its compact old centre is easy to explore on foot and is well-supplied with restaurants and bars. The city was supposedly founded by the Roman general, Pompey, and there are some exquisite Roman mosaics, plus interesting Romanesque and Gothic artefacts displayed in the fine **Museo de Navarra**.

Situated between the old and new parts of the city is Pamplona's main square, the

Plaza del Castillo – an attractive spot with shady trees, benches, a bandstand and outdoor cafés along the edges. To the northeast, the huge **cathedral** complex backs onto the city wall. Its overblown 18th-century west façade conceals a gloomy but impressive 14th- to 15th-century interior. In contrast, the beautiful Gothic cloister is an oasis of sunshine and calm, with some notable sculpture. Make sure you don't miss the **Ayuntamiento** (City Hall), a gloriously extravagant baroque confection.

Estella is an unspoiled medieval town with beautiful Romanesque buildings. 'Estella la Bella' was a favourite pilgrim stop on the road (*rúa*) to Santiago de Compostela.

On **Plaza de San Martin**, a 12th-century palace faces the church of **San Pedro de la Rúa**. The church's portal features an unusual, scalloped arch with both Moorish and Christian-inspired elements.

The Running of the Bulls

Pamplona's Fiesta de San Fermín (Festival of St Fermin), specifically the festival-time *encierro* or 'running of the bulls', so entranced the writer Ernest Hemingway that he immortalized it in his novel *The Sun Also Rises* (1926). Since his day, the *fiesta* has become an international crowd-puller, and the *encierro* is just part of the celebrations which run the gamut from wood-chopping contests to spectacular fireworks.

The *encierro* takes place daily from 7-12 July. At 8am when the bulls are released, a mass of young bloods, dressed in white with red sashes, attempt to race ahead of the bulls down the main street to the Plaza de Toros (bullring). Exciting it may be, but participants are regularly maimed and killed. The bearded Hemingway, known locally as Don Ernesto, is commemorated by a bust erected alongside the bullring.

Biblical tales carved in stone decorate the pilgrim churches on the road to Santiago.

The remains of the church's Romanesque cloister are decorated with fine carved capitals. Another noteworthy pilgrim church is the unfinished **Iglesia del Santo Sepulcro** which has a superlative Gothic portal. Across the river, the church of **San Miguel Arcangel** has a portal richly decorated with carved biblical scenes and figures designed to inspire pilgrims on their way.

Just 3km/2 miles south of Estella, the **monasterio de Irache** was another important stop on the Pilgrim Way. A Benedictine foundation, it was once a university. Its 12th-century church has an 'old' and a 'new' cloister; the latter with fine plateresque details. There

is also a wine museum where you can sample Navarrese *rosado* (rosé wine), a favourite Hemingway tipple.

You can see the high tower of the cathedral in **Tudela** from miles away, yet once you're inside the labyrinth of narrow streets you may have to seek directions. Built soon after the Reconquest on the ruins of a mosque, the 12th- to 13th-century **cathedral** is a classic of the earliest Gothic style. It boasts three monumental portals; the **Capilla de Santa Ana**, a baroque spree with flights of angels flying up the walls to the chapel's dome; and a Romanesque cloister.

The ancient, strategic town of **Sanguesa** guards a crucial bridge across the Río Aragón, which was much disputed during the struggle against the Moors, and was later a crossing point on the Pilgrim's Way.

There are many handsome medieval buildings in the town, but the *pièce de résistance* is the church of **Santa María la Real**. Its south portal is a masterpiece of stone carving decorated with biblical scenes and crowds of figures.

NORTHERN ARAGON

Mountain homeland of the medieval kings of Aragon, this sparsely populated and visually striking region really is 'undiscovered', rugged Spain. With the exception of visitors to the Ordesa National Park, foreign tourists are few and far between. The tallest peaks of all the Pyrenees belong to Aragon, and there are several good ski resorts in **Astún**, **Candanchú** and **Formigal**.

Gateway to the Aragon Pyrenees and an old stop on the Pilgrim Way, **Jaca** has been fraught with military significance for at least twelve centuries, ever since it figured in one of the earliest victories over the Moors. The enormous, low-lying 16th-century **fortress** at the edge of town is a symbol of its former strategic importance.

Jaca's other notable monument is its **cathedral**, which dates from the 11th century and is one of the oldest in Spain. Take note of its fine Romanesque frescoes, as well as Renaissance sculptures and a plateresque retable.

Ordesa National Park

Reckoned to be one of Europe's best-kept secrets, this spectacular mountain park is accessible from the village of Torla (60km/37 miles northeast of Jaca). Graceful Pyrenean chamois perch on the cliffs here, as do wild goat, roe deer, wild boar and the only ibex (a mountain goat with back-curved horns) surviving in the Pyrenees. A national park for 70 years, the dramatic 1,000m/3,250ft Ordesa valley canyon walls dwarf forests of ancient beech, silver fir and mountain pine.

You can enjoy the canyon from the comfort of your car, but to truly appreciate its beauty and scale bring hiking gear. **79**

The park information office and local stores have maps and details of suggested walks requiring varying degrees of fitness and proficiency. During summer the park can become quite busy, but snow cuts off all access from around October to April.

Zaragoza

Capital of Aragon and the one relatively big town of the region, Zaragoza can trace its origins back to the Iberians. **80** The Romans arrived in 25BC,

spanned the River Ebro with a bridge, and founded the city of Caesaraugusta. Subsequently, the Moors held the city for 400 years. The Ebro is at its best here – more than halfway from its source in the Cantabrian mountains on its way to the Mediterranean.

Backing onto the river is Zaragoza's favourite church, the cathedral-basilica of **Nuestra Señora del Pilar** (Our Lady of the Pillar). Vast and bright, it is always packed with pilgrims. According to tradition, the Virgin Mary appeared

*J*ourney's end by the Ebro for the pilgrims to Zaragoza (left); a game of petanques (below).

here in AD40, standing on the jasper column housed in the elaborate **Capilla del Pilar**. The cathedral's superb main retable is the greatest work of the sculptor Damián Forment.

The **Plaza del Pilar** has recently undergone a facelift and been expanded to become the largest square in Spain. Complete with fountains as well as floodlights, it is edged by several religious souvenir shops and outdoor cafés. Just off the plaza, the Aragon tourist office occupies the **Zuda Tower**, a 14th-century Mudéjar relic.

Zaragoza's other cathedral, **La Seo**, was built in the 12th century. Although it is mainly Gothic, the cathedral also features Romanesque remnants, Mudéjar decorations and striking baroque postscripts, plus a 17th-century belfry displaying one of the finest tapestry collections in Spain. In 1988, workmen stumbled on the site of a Roman **Forum**, built in the 3rd century, in front of the cathedral. This archaeological dig now reveals the remains of a temple, homes, shops, and offices, plus assorted statuary and general artefacts.

West of the city centre, the beautifully restored Moorish **Aljafería Palace** was founded in the 11th century, and was adapted by the Christian kings of Aragon after the Reconquest. Across the moat (now a sunken garden) you enter the world of Muslim Spain, something rarely seen this far north. **81**

Andalusia

Andalusia is an autonomous region composed of Spain's eight southernmost provinces, adding up to one-sixth of the country's total population and area. It is the home of flamenco and bullfighting, and the guardian of the Spanish soul. Andalusia's snow-clad mountains, *pueblos blancos* (white villages), olive groves and its historic Moorish cities provide an alluring backdrop to the tourist-packed highrise Costa del Sol (see p.110). This clockwise circuit of inland Andalusia starts in the hills west of Marbella.

Ronda and Jerez

Dramatically clinging to a clifftop 150m (approximately 500ft) above the Tajo gorge,

Ronda was both an Iberian and, later, a Roman settlement. Under the Moors it proved impregnable for seven centuries. The Puente Nuevo spans the gorge, which connects the new centre with the old town from where Ronda's Moorish kings and its Christian conquerors ruled at the **Palacio de Mondragón**. Behind a Renaissance portal, the elegant courtyards, horseshoe arches and Arabic inscriptions reveal the origins of this stately structure. The town's main mosque survives a short walk away as the **Santa María la Mayor** church.

Back across the bridge, seek out the neo-classical **Plaza de Toros** (bullring). It is one of the oldest in Spain and venerated as the cradle of the *corrida*. A Ronda man, Francisco Romero, spelled out the rules of bullfighting in the 18th century. There's a small museum here, which is also entertaining for the non-aficionado.

*T*ypical pueblos blancos *on a* clifftop and nestling below (left); biking in Seville (above). **83**

Old wines and young horses have brought fame to **Jerez de la Frontera**, the largest town in the province of Cádiz. The English, never very good at foreign languages, corrupted Jerez to 'sherry' and shipped out the locally produced wine by the barrel-load. Several of the many **bodegas** (wineries) in Jerez welcome tourists to their dark, aromatic halls. The helpful tourist office has details (there are no tours at weekends or during August).

As for the horses, the **Real Escuela Andaluza de Arte Ecuestre** (Royal Andalusian School of Equestrian Art) puts its star pupils through a beautifully choreographed dressage show every Thursday at noon, and there are weekday training sessions. The highlight of the equestrian calendar is the **Spring Horse Fair**, when the town is full of dandified horses and their even more elaborately dressed riders.

Below the Moorish **Alcázar** fortress, built in the 11th-century, the 18th-century **Colegiata** holds a precious image of Christ of the Vineyards. The Mudéjar church and beautiful Renaissance **chapter house** on Plaza de la Asuncion are worth a visit. There are also museums of flamenco and clocks.

Seville

Spain's fourth largest city, spirited Seville is the capital of flamenco, the birthplace of Velázquez and Murillo, a bastion of bullfighting and backdrop for the operatic temptress, Carmen. Seville has many faces: Moorish and Christian; the medieval streets of the *barrio* and impressive modern buildings erected for the EXPO '92 world fair.

In 1401, the Great Mosque of Seville was razed to make way for a colossal **cathedral** which became the largest Gothic church in the world. Its highlights include a stunning altar screen overlaid with 3,500 kilos (7,716lb) of gold; the plateresque **Capilla Real** (Royal Chapel); and, of course, the celebrated **Giralda Tower**. It is a hike up the tower's 34 stone ramps (designed for horses) and a flight of steps to the observation deck (98m/322ft) but, if you make the effort, you'll be rewarded with a tremendous panorama across the city.

Pedro the Cruel's palace, the **Alcázar**, is a sumptuous monument dating back to the 14th century. The ceilings and walls of its halls provide a magnificent concentration of Mudéjar art; and the terraced **gardens**, scattered with pools and pavilions, are an attraction in their own right.

*S*eville's landmark Giralda Tower (left); equestrian chic in Jerez de la Frontera (above).

Bordering on the Alcázar, the labyrinthine streets of the **Barrio de Santa Cruz** exude history and charm. On the border of this district more Mudéjar sensations await in the 16th-century **Casa de Pilatos**.

The royal tobacco factory where Bizet's infamous *femme fatale*, Carmen, is supposed to have rolled cigars on her thigh is now part of the **University** campus, not far from María Luisa Park. Here, the vast **85**

Seville Highlights

Alcázar, Plaza del Triunfo. Tel. 422 71 63. *Open*: Tuesday to Saturday 10.30am-5pm, Sunday 10am-1pm. *Admission*: 600 pta. Mudéjar palace with beautiful gardens. (See p.85).

Casa de Pilatos, Calle Aguilas. Tel. 422 52 98. *Open*: daily 9am-7pm for ground floor; upper storey 10am-2pm and 4pm-6pm. *Joint admission*: 1,000 pta (500 pta each). Elegant Renaissance palace-town house supposedly modelled on Pontius Pilate's house in the Holy Land. (See p.85).

Cathedral and Giralda Tower, Calle Alemanes. Tel. 456 33 21. *Open*: Monday to Saturday 11am-5pm, Sunday cathedral 2pm-4pm, Giralda 10am-4pm. *Joint admission*: 550 pta. The world's largest Gothic church and landmark Giralda Tower, a former minaret turned lofty city symbol. (See p.85).

Museo de Bellas Artes, Plaza del Museo. Tel. 422 07 90. *Open*: Tuesday to Sunday 10am-2pm. *Admission*: 250 pta. A fine collection of Spanish and foreign paintings. (See p.87).

semi-circular **Plaza de España** was constructed for the 1929 Spanish-Americas Fair. Its walls are decorated with lovely painted tiles (*azulejos*), as are the bridges across the ornamental canal. You can hire boats to be part of the scene. In the park, pavilions house the **Museo Arqueológico**, which displays many impressive remains from the Roman site of **Itálica** (a good excursion 10km/6 miles northwest) and the **Museo de Artes y Costumbres Populares** (Museum of Folk Arts and Costume).

South of the Giralda, the **Hospital de la Santa Caridad** (Holy Charity Hospital) was founded in the 17th century. The interior of its church is hung with paintings by Murillo, who also designed the dazzling *azulejos* on the exterior.

Art lovers should also visit the **Museo de Bellas Artes**.

Córdoba

Although Córdoba was once the biggest Roman city on the Iberian peninsula, today it has a strong Moorish character. By the 10th century, the capital of the caliphate was as big and brilliant as any city in Europe. It was a renowned centre of culture, science and art.

After the Reconquest, the Spaniards customarily levelled mosques and built churches on top of the rubble. In Córdoba, happily, they spared one of the world's biggest and certainly most beautiful mosques, the **Mezquita-Catedral**, so called because Charles V saw fit to build a cathedral *inside* it.

The original Great Mosque, founded in 785, grew to its present proportions under the 10th-century leader, al-Mansur. Its unprepossessing exterior gives no hint of the richness within. The dimly lit interior appears as an enchanted forest of marble, onyx and jasper columns. At the end of the main aisle, tendrils of stone twine around the 10th-century mihrab where the caliph attended to his prayers. In the very centre of the palatial mosque, the **cathedral**, a Gothic and baroque sequel, pointedly rises far above its surroundings.

Two tiers of brick and stone arches supported on a forest of 800 pillars.

Southwest of the mosque, on the river, the **Alcázar** was actually built by a Christian king, Alfonso XI. There are pleasant patios, Roman relics, terraced gardens and wonderful views from the ramparts. Across the river via the Roman bridge, the 14th-century **Torre de la Calahorra** is now a historical museum.

To absorb the full flavour of Córdoba there is no substitute for wandering the narrow streets and alleys of the **Barrio de la Judería** (Jewish Quarter), in which a small 14th-century synagogue can still be found. To the east is the town's best historical museum, the **Museo Arqueológico**. Other places of interest include the **Palacio del Marqués de Viana**, possibly one of Córdoba's finest houses, and two museums: the **Museo Taurino** (Bullfighting); and **Museo de Bellas Artes** (Fine Arts).

EAST OF CÓRDOBA

The province of Jaén, east of Córdoba, provides some of Spain's finest scenic contrasts. Here, harsh mountains stare down at gently undulating hills dotted with olive groves, and the provincial capital, **Jaén**,

*G*ranada's Moorish rulers built the imposing Alhambra (left) and Generalife gardens (below).

spreads beneath a picturesque Moorish castle, now converted to a *parador*. Jaén's sights are pretty low-key: a museum specializing in archaeological finds; a cathedral with a vast Renaissance façade; and the largest **Arab baths** in Spain.

The real reasons to venture to this little-visited region are two beautifully preserved medieval towns which flourished as Christian strongholds in the

Reconquest. **Baeza**, with more than 50 listed historical buildings, is the smaller of the two. **Úbeda** is just as engaging and its showcase square, the **Plaza Vázquez de Molina**, is surrounded by a host of magnificent Renaissance palaces (one of which has been converted to a sumptuous *parador* – see p.179) and churches. Here, the town hall is housed in the **Palacio de las Cadenas** (Palace of Chains), so called for its decoration, and the **Sacra Capilla del Salvador** (Chapel of the Holy Saviour), is the town's finest church.

Granada

The last Moorish outpost in Spain, Granada lies at the foot of the Sierra Nevada mountains. For more than two centuries (until 1492), Granada remained a self-sufficient island of Islam, where Moors, many of them craftsmen seeking safety from vanquished Córdoba and Seville, combined their talents to make medieval Granada a showcase for Moorish art. **89**

The famous **Alhambra** ('The Red One') is actually a series of palaces with its origins way back in the 9th century when the sturdy **Alcazaba** (fort) was founded. The main palace, the **Alcázar**, was constructed in the 14th century, and this is where you find the celebrated gems of Moorish architecture.

The grand tour leads via the Arabian Nights-style **Patio de los Arrayanes** (Court of the Myrtle Trees) to the **Salón de Embajadores** (Royal Audience Chamber), its walls finely decorated with filigree and calligraphy. The fountain courtyard of the **Patio de los Leones** (Court of the Lions) is edged by beautiful chambers on every side; and the writer Washington Irving once had rooms around the **Daraxa Garden** patio. Irving's *Tales from the Alhambra* (1829) revived interest in the Alhambra and helped save it from ruin.

The **Palacio de Carlos V**, a distinguished piece of Renaissance architecture, still looks like a leaden lump next to the Moorish palace. However, it houses two museums of which the **Museo Nacional de Arte Hispano-Musulmán** (the Hispano-Muslim Art) is the best, featuring exquisite examples of Moorish arts and crafts.

The Alhambra's famous gardens, the **Generalife**, surround a modest summer palace where the kings of Granada would take refuge from the pomp and protocol of the Alhambra, musing among the fountains, trees and flowers.

Facing the Alhambra hill, the **Albaicín**, Granada's oldest and most picturesque quarter, is fun to explore, affording glimpses of the Alhambra between whitewashed houses, outdoor restaurants and cafés. At the bottom of the hill are some **Arab baths** which are rarely visited.

In the town centre, Granada's white and gold cathedral stands next to the **Capilla Real**, a Renaissance masterpiece built to house the white marble tombs of the Catholic Monarchs, Ferdinand and Isabella, their daughter Joanna the Mad, and her husband Philip the Fair. Amongst the

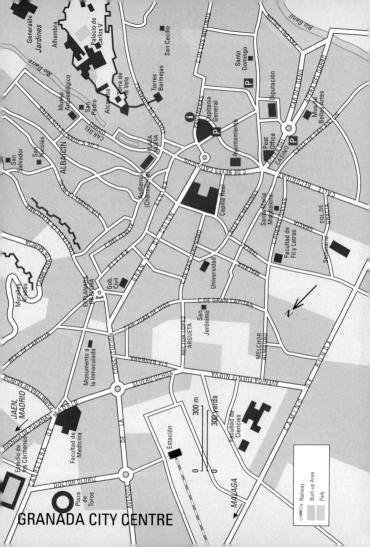

GRANADA CITY CENTRE

treasures in the sacristy are Ferdinand's sword and Isabella's crown, plus superb works of art from Isabella's personal collection.

Sierra Nevada and the Alpujarras

About an hour's drive south of Granada, the road across the Sierra Nevada mountains rises to over 3,352m (11,000ft), making it Europe's highest

navigable road (summer only). It's quite a test of driving and the views are tremendous, but the goal for most visitors who come this way is the ski resort of **Sol y Nieve**. There is a ski jump here, but the amenities are more suitable for beginners or intermediate skiers.

The Alpujarras mountains are the south-facing slopes of the Sierra Nevada. They are probably the wildest part of all southern Spain, and it was here that the Moors made their final retreat after the fall of Granada. Consequently, the villages look as Moorish as the *pueblos blancos* in the lower valleys. Do pay a visit to **Bubión** and, especially, **Capileira**, which has already been 'discovered' to a small degree.

If you are the active sort, this is marvellous hiking country, from a gentle ramble to serious climbing. Horse riding is another speciality of the area.

Grafted onto the hillside, mountain villages endure baking summers and freezing winters.

Extremadura

The harsh, open landscape of the Spanish west is as beautiful as it is unyielding, and the southern portion, known as Extremadura (the 'land beyond the Río Duero'), is one of the least visited regions of Spain. Extremadura reached a brief zenith during Roman times, when a provincial capital was established at Mérida, but its real fame comes from being the 'Cradle of the *Conquistadores*', the adventurers who colonized the new continent of the Americas.

FROM SOUTH TO NORTH

Zafra is the most attractive of southern Extremadura's towns – its white houses converging on two arcaded plazas recalling its Moorish origins. So, too, does the design of the medieval Alcázar, now a sumptuous *parador*, where adventurer Hernán Cortés stayed before setting off to conquer Mexico.

The gateway to Portugal, built-up **Badajoz** is the biggest city in Extremadura. The ancient **Puerta de Palmas** fortified city gate leads into the medieval walled city. Another arch used to bar the way to the **citadel** overlooking the Guadiana river, where the rulers of the Moorish kingdom of Badajoz held sway.

With its heavy walls and pinnacled tower, the **cathedral** was founded in the 13th century, and is largely Gothic with Renaissance additions. Inside are impressive choir stalls, paintings, tapestries and tombstones. The **Museo Provincial de Bellas Artes**, which exhibits some good Flemish tapestries, is on the same square.

Today, **Mérida** is a sleepy modern town, but once it was an imperial capital dubbed the 'Rome of Spain', and it can still lay claim to the greatest number of Roman remains in any Spanish town.

The *pièce de résistance* is the partially restored 1st-century BC **Teatro Romano** with seating for more than 5,500 spectators. In summer, Greek and Roman plays are produced here. The elliptical **Anfiteatro** **93** next door (also known as the Circus Maximus), was designed to hold 15,000 spectators for gladiatorial contests and chariot races. At times it was even flooded to host recreations of great naval battles.

Don't miss the award-winning **Museo Nacional de Arte Romano**. Its beautifully displayed collections include examples of Roman statuary, locally minted coins and paintings discovered on the podium of the arena. Around town are many other Roman monuments: a temple to Diana; Trajan's Arch; an aqueduct; and a 0.8km (half-mile) bridge spanning the Guadiana.

*F*rancisco Pizarro, the man who conquered Peru, riding high over Trujillo's Plaza Mayor.

From afar, the turrets, spires and crenellations of the rambling **Monasterio de Nuestra Señora de Guadalupe** announce an impressive shrine. From nearby, it overwhelms the tiny town of **Guadalupe** spread at its feet. Surrounded by a huddle of small streets and squares, the monastery is Spain's fourth most important pilgrim site and guardian of a precious wooden statue of the Virgin of Guadalupe, patron saint of the *conquistadores*.

New World gold paid for the construction of the huge monastery complex, covering an area of about 2ha (5 acres). It's an architectural hybrid with a flamboyant façade flanked by stern defensive towers, Mudéjar and Gothic cloisters, and a church founded in the 14th century and enlarged four centuries later. Guided tours (generally in Spanish) visit the cloisters, an embroidery museum, chapter house, and sacristy, housing a remarkable collection of paintings by Zurbarán, among others.

Seen from afar, the hilltop skyline of **Trujillo** is one of those magical sights sure to revive the spirits of any weary traveller. Although Spain has historic towns with far more imposing architectural monuments, Trujillo is a beauty, and a worthy monument to its *conquistadore* patrons.

The eccentrically shaped **Plaza Mayor** is a happy meeting place of distinguished and ordinary buildings. On the southwest corner, the **Palacio del Marqués de la Conquista** was built by a renowned local soldier, Hernando Pizarro. An equestrian statue of his half-brother Francisco stands on the square.

Sons of Trujillo

Of all the *conquistador* towns, none is more proud of its sons' exploits than Trujillo. The most famous were the Pizarros, who conquered Peru, but other natives were Diego García Paredes and Francisco de las Casas, who both founded towns called Trujillo in Venezuela and Honduras respectively, and Francis Orellana, the first European navigator of the Amazon.

Diego García in particular had a fearsome reputation. He was known as the Extremadura Samson and among his legendary feats of strength he is said to have picked up the font in Santa María la Mayor to carry holy water to his mother. The tombs of the Pizarros and that of García can be seen in the same church.

There are half a dozen other palaces around the town, decorated with heroic portals, historic escutcheons and pretty patios – all worthy of investigation. Storks' nests crown the clock tower over the Gothic church of **San Martín**, which has a long, dark nave paved with ancient tombstones.

The Romanesque and Gothic church of **Santa María la Mayor** boasts a fine Hispano-Flemish style retable. The two imposing stone seats on the balcony were built for Spain's Catholic monarchs, Ferdinand and Isabella. There are marvellous views from the heavily fortified **castillo** on the hilltop, which began as a Roman fort and later became a Moorish *alcazaba*. Above the keyhole-shaped main gate, a niche contains a statue of the Virgin of Victory, the local patron saint. The view over Trujillo from here is the best in town.

Once a Roman settlement, the walled city of **Cáceres** offers a magnificent assembly of mellow stone churches, palaces and towers. A provincial **96** capital and college town, it is much livelier than Trujillo. The **Plaza Mayor** is the hub of local life, especially during the evening *paseo* when the historic buildings are illuminated, providing a dignified backdrop to the relaxed ritual.

Cáceres' skyline is a forest of towers, a popular feature with the local stork population. One of the most visible examples is part of the Toledo-Moctezuma mansion, formerly home to a follower of Cortés who married the daughter of the Aztec emperor.

Go through the Arco de la Estrella (Star Arch) into the **Old Town** and wander down the warren of streets lined with imposing buildings sporting ostentatious heraldic shields. The Casa de las Veletas (Weathervane House) has been turned into an excellent **provincial museum** featuring archaeological finds, displays of historical costumes and local customs.

In its day, the magnificent six-arched **Roman bridge** over the Tagus near **Alcántara** was a world-renowned engineering feat. No less than

194m (636ft) long, with extraordinarily high arches, it is altogether so impressive that the town was named after it: in Arabic *al-Qantara* means 'the bridge'.

East of Alcántara, the Tagus has been dammed, giving the landscape a dramatic facelift. Besides its aesthetic contribution, the lake is also a popular recreation area.

When Alfonso VIII of Castile liberated the hilltop town of **Plasencia** from the Moors in the 12th century, he fortified it with a city wall defended by 68 towers. The town's importance has since diminished, but the bristling silhouette is still impressive and Plasencia's aristocratic mansions and historic churches retain their allure.

The **cathedral** works its architectural way from Romanesque to Gothic. There are plateresque embellishments on the exterior and the choir stalls, illustrating biblical stories and scenes from medieval life, are particularly notable.

In the Castilian province of Salamanca, **La Alberca** is a national monument with a difference. This modest rural village is Old Spain personified. Heavily-loaded donkeys clatter down the main street; simple, whitewashed homes cram into alleys, their flimsy-looking wooden balconies weighed down by flowerpots; and the bean harvest is dried in the Plaza Pública. The highlight of the local calendar is the Feast of the Assumption (August 15), when the entire population turns out in traditional costume to celebrate.

You can walk all the way around the hill town of **Ciudad Rodrigo** in no time. Just take the 2km (1-mile) path which follows the medieval defences past the old castle (now a *parador*).

There are some dozen worthy old mansions in town, most with interesting stone carvings and perhaps an inviting patio. The Plaza Mayor is distinguished by the **Casa Consistoral** (Town Hall), a 16th-century arcaded palace with a belfry, while the exterior of the **cathedral** is full of fine sculptural details.

97

The Costas

From the Costa Brava at the eastern end of the Pyrenees, all the way round to the Costa de la Luz and the border with Portugal, the famous Spanish *costas* attract millions of holidaymakers every year. The coastline stretches for some 2,500km (1,562 miles), from the sheltered Mediterranean to the blustery Atlantic. There are rocky coves and glorious strands of golden sand; family resorts and jet-set ports. In spite of the much-reported ravages of extensive development and building, you can still find many charming spots along the coast. The *costas*' generally cheap and cheerful, sun and fun atmosphere will always be a major attraction.

*T*he coves and rock pools of the Costa Brava (below); laid-back and carefree (right).

COSTA BRAVA

Perhaps the prettiest coastline in Spain until package tourism arrived here in the early 1960s, the cliffs and coves of the 'Rugged Coast' still conceal a handful of traditional fishing villages and secluded beaches in the north of the region. You will find the major tourism development concentrated in the south (at the Lloret de Mar resort, for instance).

Cadaqués may look like the typical Spanish, whitewashed fishermen's village, but it attracts a distinctly atypical kind of crowd of chic, monied holidaymakers. Although it is still a working port, without a decent beach, the village has developed into something of an artists' haunt. In fact, in 1929, Salvador Dalí built a modest retreat here on the edge of Cadaqués at Port Lligat.

On top of the old town, the 17th-century **church**, with a rich altarpiece, was built as a replacement for its predecessor, burned down in 1543 by Barbarossa, the infamous Barbary pirate. Art enthusiasts can admire a selection of modern masters in the **Perrot-Moore Museum** (founded by Dalí's ex-secretary); and the local

Museu d'Art also includes works by household names.

Ampurias was built by the Greeks, improved by the Iberians and then greatly expanded by the Romans. The site was perpetually occupied for some 1,500 years. An archaeologists delight, excavations have uncovered the remains of villas, temples and marketplaces of the different civilizations. You will also find lovely sea views.

The most sensational find was a statue of Asclepius, the Greek god of medicine, which **99** was sculpted in marble from an Athenian quarry. The original has been removed to Barcelona, but a copy stands in the ruined temple. The on-site **museum** displays local finds from ceramics and jewels to household items and weapons.

In the dramatic cliff country south of Bagur, **Tossa de Mar** was an artists' colony before it metamorphosed into a fully developed international resort. The town remains surprisingly attractive, its **Vila Vella** (Old Town) enclosed by brooding 12th-century walls and guarded by three great towers. The **museum** here boasts paintings by Marc Chagall and other artists who visited the town.

Gerona (Girona) is the inland gateway to the Costa Brava, and is a pleasant day trip destination from the coast (30km/20 miles west). The old town is fun to explore, with its typical medieval streets such as **Carrer de la Força**, once the heart of the Jewish quarter. Gerona's Gothic **cathedral** is said to have the widest nave in

Dalí in Figueres

Born in Figueres (Figueras) (30km/19 miles west of Cadaqués), in 1904, the Surrealist artist Salvador Dalí endowed his home town with the suitably surreal Teatre-Museu Dalí (closed Monday). The second-most visited museum in Spain (after the Prado), it is a typically outrageous Dalíesque project. A municipal theatre was gutted, its stage filled with bizarre sculptures, and an ancient Cadillac was parked on the patio supporting a statue of a gilt-breasted Amazon. There are giant models of hens' eggs on the battlements, a roofline topped by a geodesic dome, and Dalí's version of the Sistine Chapel – a homage to Mae West with her lips replaced by a voluptuous red sofa. Shocks and jokes aside, however, the museum represents an intriguing cross-section of Dalí's work.

the world at 22m (72ft), and the **treasury**, Museu Capitular, is crammed with precious gold- and silverwork, rare illuminated manuscripts, statuary and tapestries. Close by, the 12th-century **Banys Arabs** (Arab Baths) are the best preserved in Spain after those found at Granada.

*A*rtists, not sunseekers, flock to the beachless fishing port of Cadaqués.

COSTA DORADA

The Costa Dorada derives its name from the fine golden (*daurada*) sand beaches which stretch almost without a break for 241km (150 miles) south of Barcelona. the city of Tarragona, midway down the coast, is covered in *Around Barcelona* (see p.48).

The sophisticated and attractive resort of **Sitges** retains much of its old-world charm. The old town is built around a promontory. Surmounting this,

the neo-Gothic **Palau Mar i Cel** (Palace of the Sea and Sky) houses a fine collection of paintings and *objets d'art* from around the world plus romantic sea views through picture windows.

Adjacent, **Cau Ferrat** (iron lair) is one of Spain's most exquisite small museums. Works by El Greco and Picasso, ceramics, crystal and much more are imaginatively displayed. Another good museum is the **Museu Romàntic**, in an aristocratic mansion lavishly decorated in 19th-century style.

*M*elimato (cheese and honey) is a favourite Catalan dessert; Palau Mar i Cel, Sitges.

By far the biggest resort on the Costa Dorada, **Salou** has few pretensions. It is a well-ordered, no-frills playground for north European package holidaymakers offering them huge beaches and a good range of facilities and entertainment.

Salou also boasts a brand-new theme park, the **Port Aventura**, which promises a journey of adventure through exotic lands, plus all sorts of rides, restaurants and live entertainment. During the early evening, crowds assemble to watch the town's **illuminated fountain**, designed by Carlos Buigas, who is also renowned for the famous 'dancing fountains' in Barcelona.

Salou's more classy neighbour is an attractive fishing port turned resort. **Cambrils** has a long seafront and a charming oddity in its large fleet of *bous* – small fishing boats carrying somewhat over-sized lamps for night duty. Their daily catch is bought up by the many good waterfront **fish restaurants**. Cambrils is a Catalan gourmet town with a garland of Michelin stars.

The Ebro Delta

The Ebro delta is the largest wetlands in Catalonia and, after France's famous Camargue, the most important aquatic environment in the western Mediterranean. It is a major breeding ground for waders, waterfowl and sea birds. Some 7,700ha (19,000 acres) of the delta wetlands have been set aside as a protected National Park truly making this a birdwatcher's paradise.

There is a tourist office at **Deltebre** which can supply general information, maps, details of boat excursions and birdwatching sites. Non-birdwatchers can enjoy the wide open spaces, the glittering green rice paddies (the basic ingredient for *paella* is grown here), and glimpses of the sleepy rural lifestyle.

103

Tortosa held a key strategic role for centuries as the last major town before the sea, guarding the Ebro river. The

fortress at the top of the town, **La Zuda**, was built by the Moors. Later it became a royal residence of the Aragonese kings. The **cathedral** in the old town was built between the 14th and 16th centuries, and is a fine example of Catalan Gothic. Inside is a beautiful triptych and two carved stone pulpits.

*R*ice paddies in the Ebro delta (left); the Gothic bulwark of Tortosa Cathedral (below).

COSTA DEL AZAHAR

The 'Orange Blossom Coast' begins south of the Tarragona provincial border and stretches for 112km (70 miles) down a section of coast well-endowed with beaches backed by citrus groves and olive orchards.

Crowned by a medieval castle, picturesque **Peñíscola** is built on a rocky promontory jutting out into the sea. Its sloping streets of whitewashed houses are regularly invaded by tourists, but it's still a pretty place, and looks even better when it's floodlit at night.

The **castle**, built by the Knights Templar on the ruins of a Moorish fortress, has two claims to fame: Pope Benedict XIII found asylum here after being dismissed from his position until his death in 1423; and the castle featured in the film *El Cid*, starring Charlton Heston. There's a museum and terrific sea views from the restored ramparts.

To the north, there are two popular but far less crowded fishing port-cum-beach resorts in **Benicarló** and **Vinaroz**.

The nine-month siege of **Sagunto** (Roman *Saguntum*) by the Carthaginian general Hannibal in 219BC, ignited the Second Punic War. The inhabitants burnt the city and themselves to avoid capture, but when *Saguntum* was eventually retaken, the Romans redeveloped it on a grand scale.

Today, Sagunto's Roman monuments include the heavily restored **Roman theatre**. Nearby, a modest archaeological museum exhibits Iberian, Roman and medieval relics. From the hilltop **acropolis**, known as Castell de Sagunt, sweeping views reach over the citrus orchards to the sea.

Valencia

Lapped by an ocean of orange trees, Valencia is Spain's third-biggest city. Its crowded historic centre is framed by parks and gardens. Valencia was founded by the Romans in 138BC and it later flourished as the capital of a far-flung Moorish kingdom until El Cid captured it at the end of the 11th century. **105**

*A*rabs *introduced azulejos (decorative ceramic tiles) to Spain in the 12th century.*

No sooner had Christianity been restored than plans were laid for the cathedral, **La Seo**. A patchwork of architectural styles, its landmark octagonal Gothic tower, known as the *Miguelete* or *Micalet*, is a symbol of the city.

Valencia's **Longa de la Seda** (Silk Exchange), built in the 15th-century, is a masterpiece. Here, silk merchants once did business. Across the street, the Moderniste-style **106**

central market (built in 1928) is a colourful cornucopia of comestibles – fruit, vegetables, fish and meat destined for the city's kitchens.

Valencia boasts several museums. The **Museo Nacional de Cerámica**, housed in an astonishing old palace, has assembled hundreds of glorious glazed tiles (*azulejos*) amongst its treasures. The city's major art collection, at the **Museo Provincial de Bellas Artes**, exhibits paintings by Bosch, El Greco, Goya and Velázquez and has a definitive collection of 15th-century Valencian art.

Gandía

A town in two parts, Gandía has a busy resort on a vast beach down on the coast, and a splendid 14th-century palace tucked away in its inland town centre. Birthplace of Duke Francisco de Borja, 16th-century noble turned Jesuit priest, the **Palacio de los Duques** is now a showcase for splendid tapestries, paintings and antiques, many of them amassed by the pious duke.

COSTA BLANCA

Named *Akra Leuka* (White Headland) by ancient Greek tradesmen who founded a colony here 2,500 years ago, the brilliant light, hot, dry climate and miles of fine, sandy beaches and temperate water make the 'White Coast' one of Spain's liveliest tourist zones.

The Northern Beaches

The beaches sprawl to the north and south of the town of **Denia**, named after a Roman temple dedicated to the goddess Diana. Further south, the family resort of **Jávea** has a fine beach and a pleasant old quarter; **Calpe** is a former fishing village with pleasant sandy beaches in the lee of the **Peñón de Ifach**, an imposing volcanic outcrop; and **Altea's** old houses climb steeply to a carefully preserved old quarter virtually unchanged in the face of the tourist tide and home to a thriving artistic community.

The very name **Benidorm** has come to symbolize the worst excesses of package tourism. There is a skyline akin to Manhattan, and high season queues to get on to the beach – all 7km (4 miles) of it! But Benidorm knows what the package-tour invaders want – and provides it cheerfully and efficiently, round the clock and without pretension.

Surprisingly, the old fishermen's quarter still exists and is a major saving grace. Likewise, there are sweeping views from the attractive **Balcón de Mer** encompassing the town's truly impressive crescent of beaches backed by the wind-sculpted mountains.

Just offshore, boats visit the **Isla de Benidorm**, a bird sanctuary; and the Moorish eagles' nest village-fortress of **Castell de Guadalest**, situated 28km/17 miles northwest, is a favourite excursion.

With a population of over a quarter of a million, **Alicante** is a typical bustling Mediterranean port with a splendid palm-lined promenade, lots of outdoor cafés and surprisingly few foreign tourists. The spacious beach of Playa Postiguet is a bonus.

Alicante's imposing clifftop **Castillo de Santa Barbara** was built on the site of a Carthaginian fort founded in the 3rd century BC. Below the castle, the old **Barrio de Cruz** is atmospheric and full of character. Here, you will find the baroque façade of the 14th-century church of **Santa María**, next to the **Museo de Arte de Siglo XX** (Museum of 20th-Century Art), focussing on Spanish artists: Miró, Picasso and Dalí.

On many road signs, the town of Elche appears as a terse Elx, which is what the Moors called it. **Elche** is famous for is its **date plantation**, the largest in Europe. The **Parque Municipal** is shaded by superb palms (naturally) as well as a citrus alley and a noisy frog pond. The tourist office is on the edge of the park which is bordered by a group of fine historic buildings, including the **Palacio de Altamira**, a former royal holiday residence, and now occupied by an archaeological museum. The museum has a replica of the famous *Dama de Elche* sculpture; the original is in Madrid. There are yet more palms in Elche's prettiest precinct, the **Hort del Cura** (Priest's Garden), as well as pomegranates, orange trees and a small forest of cacti.

The historic fortifications on the seafront make good vantage points along the coast.

COSTA CÁLIDA

The southern portion of the Costa Blanca is known as the Costa Cálida (Warm Coast). Its most famous stretch is the **Mar Menor** (Little Sea), a vast lagoon almost completely sheltered from the Mediterranean by a 22km (14-mile) spit. High-rise resort facilities have multiplied on the sandy breakwater, including the famous Club La Manga holiday sports complex.

Cartagena, named after the Carthaginians, is an important port and naval base with a well-protected harbour overlooked by the ruins of the 14th-century **Castillo de la Concepción**. It's worth driving up here for the views. Then take a stroll around the old town down to the port. On the front is a submarine directly from the pages of a Jules Verne novel, built by local inventor, Isaac Peral in 1888.

The inland capital of the Costa Cálida, **Murcia** is pleasant and prosperous with a pretty old town. The landmark **Catedral de Santa María**, built in the 14th-century, is one of Spain's finest, adorned with a fabulous baroque façade. The outstanding **Vélez chapel** is a highlight of the interior, and in the museum there are wood sculptures by Francisco Salzillo (1797-1883), Murcia's greatest artist. There are more of his works in the **Museo Salzillo**. Among Murcia's other museums, the **Museo Provincial de Bellas Artes** (Fine Arts) is the best.

COSTA DE ALMERÍA

This is Spain's dustbowl. A searing and parched corner of the Mediterranean coast, development has been kept at bay until very recently. The fledgling resorts of **Mojácar**, **Roquetas da Mar** and **Garruche** lie just inside the borders of Andalusia. Inland, the dramatic, desolate, desert-like landscape is a favourite with spaghetti-Western film-makers, who have nicknamed it **Mini-Hollywood**.

A modern city, **Almería** reveals its Moorish origins in the huge 8th-century **Alcazaba** **109**

*B*usiness as usual in the old town (above); a racier lifestyle awaits at the marina (right).

fortress which overhangs the town and port. The city's crenellated outer walls and a section of the turreted ramparts remain standing amongst the 35ha (87 acres) of ruins.

The waterfront **Paseo de Almería** is ideal for strolling and shopping. Just inland from the harbour, the fortified Gothic **cathedral** was completed in the mid-16th century.

COSTA DEL SOL

West of Almería, the famed 'Sunshine Coast' unfurls in a dense strip of resorts, hotels, *urbanizaciones*, holiday villages and timeshare developments spilling onto less than impressive beaches. However, with an estimated 326 days of sunshine per year, everybody wants a piece of the action and a place in the sun – right from the package tourist to the rich and famous.

East of Málaga, **Nerja** is the only sizeable resort of note, and is popular with holidaymakers who can still discern a hint of old Spain. Hotels cluster around Nerja's clifftop **Balcón de Europa**, an attractive palm-fringed promenade.

The area's principal attraction is the **Cueva de Nerja**, a truly cavernous cave 4km (2.5 miles) east of town. Wall paintings and archaeological finds indicate that the stalactite-encrusted cave (home to the world's longest stalactite at 59m/195ft) has been inhabited intermittently since the days of Cro-Magnon man.

Málaga – the busiest airport gateway in the region, but rarely penetrated by tourists – has a busy harbour overlooked by an **Alcazaba**, built by the Moors. Ramps and pathways lead up through the attractive landscaped ruins to a modest archaeological museum. At the top of the hill, the sprawling **Gibralfaro** fort affords spectacular views out to sea and inland to the mountains.

Situated a short distance from Málaga's grandiose but rather gloomy cathedral, the **Museo de Bellas Artes** has a worthy assortment of Spanish paintings and a room devoted to Picasso, who was born nearby at Plaza de la Merced 15. The traditional costumes and folk arts displayed in the entertaining **Museo Artes y Costumbres Populares** are well worth a quick detour. They are housed in an inn, built in the 17th century near the Guadalmedina riverbed.

Known as 'T-Town' to fans, **Torremolinos** is the official fun capital of the Costa del Sol. The old town is not altogether unattractive, and locals (many of them ex-patriates) take good care of package tourist business. A few local fishermen still put to sea in gaily painted wooden *barques* from **La Carihuela** beach, and then unload their catch into the lively beachfront restaurants.

The adjacent resort of **Fuengirola** is a similarly popular place, but more family orientated than Torremolinos.

The aristocrat of the Costa del Sol resorts, royalty and

celebrities have gravitated to **Marbella** for decades. As a result, prices are higher here than anywhere else along the coast, but standards of accommodation, service and cuisine are superior, too.

The 28km (17-mile) beachfront is built up with expensive hotel complexes, and the spacious **marina** sees more than its fair share of luxury pleasure craft. Across the main road, the **old town** is an attractive warren of twisting streets and alleys full of shops, restaurants and the odd historic church.

Puerto Banús is Spain's answer to Saint-Tropez. This chic 1970s marina-shopping-entertainment complex is full of tasteful bars, pricey boutiques, classy restaurants and nightclubs. Its waterfront parade is a catwalk for 'beautiful people', many of whom arrive aboard the massive yachts berthed in the harbour.

Colourful local markets and roadside stalls offer tasty regional produce bargains.

The last of the big resorts on the western flank of the coast, **Estepona** provides all the essentials for a sporty, modern holiday – beaches, golf courses, marina – all in an engaging small-town atmosphere. Of Roman origin, Estepona preserves the remains of Moorish fortifications and watchtowers.

COSTA DE LA LUZ

The Atlantic-facing coast of southern Spain, the 'Coast of Light', receives a mere trickle of tourists compared with the bustling Costa del Sol. It is extremely blustery and tourist facilities are limited, but to make up for that, there are long, uncrowded beaches, easy access to Seville, and Spain's best national park (see p.115).

The windsurfing capital of Europe, **Tarifa** is just 13km (8 miles) across the water from North Africa. Morocco's Rif mountains hang on the horizon, and Tangier is often clearly visible. Parts of Tarifa's old Moorish walls still stand, as does a 10th-century fortress, the **Castillo de Guzmán el** **113**

Bueno. Accomplished windsurfers revel in the ideal gusty conditions at **Tarifa beach** (9km/5.5 miles west).

Cádiz

Rolling Atlantic waves crash against the rocky defences of this narrow peninsula city, basking in the sunshine. Its protected harbour was settled by Phoenician traders around 3,000 years ago, making it one of the world's oldest cities. Christopher Columbus set out on his second and fourth voyages to the Americas from here. Later, Cádiz grew rich on the New World trade, and attracted the attention of Sir Francis Drake, whose 1587 attack on the city 'singed the king of Spain's beard'.

A 'salty seadog' sort of place, Cádiz has an **old town** district which is well-supplied with shops and outdoor cafés. The excellent **Museo de Cádiz** exhibits Phoenician and Roman artefacts, paintings by Zurbarán, as well as local crafts. Overlooking the ocean, the baroque **cathedral** has a landmark dome glittering like gold in the sunshine, and a lavish treasury.

Situated at the mouth of the Guadalquivir river on the Atlantic coast, **Sanlúcar** is a popular getaway for families from Seville. The town is also famed for its vineyards which produce the grapes for *Manzanilla*, a rich wine similar to sherry. The sea breezes are supposed to supply *Manzanilla's* distinctive salty tang.

Doñana National Park

The largest and most famous of Spain's national parks, this wild conservation zone is made up of three environments: sand dunes (where parts of *Lawrence of Arabia* were filmed), pine woodlands and marshes. More than 250 bird species can be seen here, including rarities such as purple gallinule, imperial eagle and crested coot. Mongoose, deer, wild boar and Iberian lynx also roam free.

You can only visit the park by guided tour from the reception centre at El Acebuche. For further details and reservations, phone (955) 43 04 32 as far in advance as possible.

*F*our-hour safari tours can only explore a small fraction of the 173,000-acre Doñana reserve.

The Islands

Spain's alluring island archipelagos have both received mediocre press in recent years due to over-development, but you have only to look beyond this to find wonderful scenery, vibrant local colour, tranquility and peace. In the western Mediterranean, the Balearics comprise a sunny cross-section of landscapes from mountainous Majorca to low-slung, sleepy Formentera. The volcanic Canaries in the Atlantic, just off the coast of North Africa, thrive as a semi-tropical escape for those in search of winter sun. Within each of the archipelagos, every island has its own character.

THE BALEARICS

 ## Majorca

For decades, Majorca (*Mallorca* in Spanish) has been Europe's playground. The largest tourism concentration in the world focuses on the southern Bay of Palma and, to a lesser extent, on the northern Bay of Alcudia. Outside these areas, there's still plenty of unspoiled Majorca to delight in and the scenery is fantastic.

The island measures 72km (45 miles) by 96km (60 miles), and well over half of the total population lives in the animated and cosmopolitan capital city of **Palma de Mallorca**. Palma's tree-shaded central promenade, **Es Born** (the islanders speak a Mallorquí dialect of Catalan), is the hub of the city's social life.

Rebuilt for the medieval kings of Majorca after the Reconquest, the **Palacio Almudaina** now houses a local history museum in one wing of the palace. Overshadowing the palace's delicately arched and covered balconies, the magnificent Gothic cathedral, **La Seu**, founded in 1299, is more than a match for anything the mainland can offer. For great

The end of the road: Cabo Formentor at the northern tip of Majorca.

views, head for the cylindrical keep of **Castillo de Bellver**, which has commanded the land and sea approaches to the city since the 14th century.

Exploring Majorca's 965km (600-mile) coastline clockwise from Palma, **Port d'Andratx** lies close to the western tip of the island, on a sheltered bay popular with yachtsmen. Near **Banyalbufar**, place of some of the finest terraces on the island, is **La Granja**, a cross between a stately home, craft centre, traditional farmhouse and museum of rural life.

Frédéric Chopin and George Sand stayed at the monastery of **Sa Cartuja**, near Valldemosa, in 1838-9. Today, coachloads of curious visitors descend on the monastery to see the garden suite the couple rented, and displays of related memorabilia. **Deía**, a pretty hilltop town built with honey-coloured stone, is probably the island's most attractive town and a good base for visiting the **Tranmuntana** region in the northwest. A favourite haunt of the independent traveller, there are few beaches

*P*alma's historic Castillo de Bellver (left); Mallorcans dancing in the street (below).

here, but a spectacular (if hairraising) corniche road affords magnificent views.

The town of **Sóller** is linked to Palma by a delightful narrow-gauge railway. Its polished wood carriages make the hour-long journey through orchards and terrific mountain scenery. An old San Francisco-style open tram then travels the short journey down to the seaside and the pretty harbour of Port de Sóller.

Port de Pollença is the sort of seaside resort that has given Majorca a good name, with its lovely beach and inoffensive accommodation. A road runs from here to the cliffs of **Cabo Formentor**, the northernmost projection of the island.

The most popular tourist excursion on Majorca is a trip to the caves peppering the east coast. A two-hour guided tour of the **Cuevas del Drach** (Dragon's Caves) takes in all sorts of dramatically lit formations. It is said the **Cuevas de Artá** so impressed and inspired author Jules Verne, that he went off and wrote *Journey to the Centre of the Earth*.

Minorca

Minorca (*Menorca* in Spanish) is one-fifth the area of Majorca, and receives a fraction of the visitors. A tranquil, low-key island, Minorca's main tourist development is in the west. The north is more scenic but many beaches, both to the **119** north and south, can only be reached on foot or by four-wheel drive vehicle.

The main town and deep-water habour of **Mahón** (*Maó* in Menorquí) was occupied by the British for a large part of the 18th century. The little city clusters on the cliffs above the port, and buildings in the older quarter of town have a distinctly Georgian appearance. A boat trip around the harbour makes a fun excursion.

Ciudadela (*Ciutadella*), on the west coast, also has a fine harbour, but is more akin to Andalusia than old England. **Ses Arcades**, the street leading to the Gothic cathedral built in the 14th century, is all arch-ways and completely Moorish. Visit the **city museum** in the town hall (*Ayuntamiento*) for its rather curious rag-bag of is-land history.

The best beach and resort on the island is **Cala Santa Gal-dana**, a beautiful horseshoe-shaped cove developed in a restrained fashion. **Fornells**, on the north coast, is another relaxed resort and still an active fishing port.

Ibiza

A long-time favourite of Europe's hippies, Ibiza now caters to the seriously hip from assorted rock stars and artists to plane-loads of dance-crazy youths who pack the high-rise hotels and nightspots of the is-land's busiest resort develop-ment at San Antonio Abad.

Beyond the beaches and marathon parties, **Ibiza Town** (*Eivissa*), the island's capital, is lovely. Its ancient walled town, **Dalt Vila**, is a cobbled maze on a hillside packed with whitewashed houses, tiny bars, shops, flea markets and restau-rants serving local fare.

The capital has two **archae-ological museums** boasting a treasury of Carthaginian art. One, the Puig des Molins, is built adjacent to a necropolis, and tours of the burial cham-bers are given.

The beaches start immedi-ately south of town, but the best, and certainly the trendi-est, on the island are generally agreed to be those at **Las Sali-nas**. Other good spots include **Portinatx** and **San Miguel** in the north. You can see regular displays of folk dancing and visit caves at San Miguel.

Formentera

The 11km (7-mile) sea voyage from Ibiza takes 75 minutes by boat, or around half that by hydrofoil. Either way, it's often a bumpy ride. There is no airport here, and very little water, which has hindered any large-scale development. Building on Formentera is restricted to a maximum of four storeys.

Once the sole retreat of the backpacker and laid-back beach bum, Formentera is now catering for package tourists. They come for much the same reasons – unimpaired horizons and endless uncommercialized nudist beaches. Windsurfing aside, there is little to do here but relax.

Ibiza Town: crowned by the cathedral and 16th-century walls of the Dalt Vila.

THE CANARY ISLANDS

Tenerife

The largest of the Canaries, Tenerife can offer more attractions and more contrasts than any of its island neighbours. The busiest local package tourism destinations are **Los Cristianos** and **Playa de Las Américas** in the southwest.

Santa Cruz de Tenerife (northeast) is the capital and administrative centre of the westerly Canaries. Though not a beauty, it has undeniable Spanish charm and several picturesque squares and gardens such as flower-bedecked **Plaza Weyler** at the end of Calle Castillo, the main shopping street. A short walk away, the **Parque García Sanabria** is famous for its fountains and floral clock.

The city's best museum is the **Museo Municipal de Bellas Artes**, which displays some fine Spanish and Flemish works. The adjacent church of San Francisco is also worth a

visit. Close to the seafront, the **Iglesia Matriz de la Concepción** dates from the 16th century and contains historical relics, such as Nelson's faded battle flag. North of town, the island's best beach, **Las Teresitas**, stretches in a golden crescent of Saharan sand for almost 1.5km (1 mile).

Mount Teide, Tenerife, the tallest mountain in Spain (left); a tall order of local flowers (below).

On the north coast, **Puerto de la Cruz** is a popular resort where the lack of a decent beach has been remedied by the wonderful **Lago de Martiánez**. This 3ha (8-acre) seafront complex has swimming lagoons and sunbathing terraces which are landscaped with palms.

The charming pedestrianized street of **Calle de San Telmo** descends into town, passing the majestic 17th-century **Iglesia de la Peña de Francia** (Church of the Rock of France). The many cafés, restaurants and shops on **Plaza Charco**, the main square, are busy at all hours.

At **Loro Parque**, the world's largest collection of parrots (over 230 species) is on show in beautiful sub-tropical gardens. Other attractions include flamingos and performing dolphins. The oldest local attraction is undoubtedly the **Jardín Botánico**, founded by royal decree in 1788, and located on the road to Orotava. On the same road, **Banañera El Guanche** is a working banana plantation with a great **123**

*T*oucans come and go as they please at Palmito Park (above); a courtyard oasis (right).

Don't miss the 17th-century **Casa de Los Balcones** (House of the Balconies) with its lovely courtyard, restored apartments and handicraft displays.

The highlight of the island in every sense is **Mount Teide**, a volcanic cone in the Las Cañadas del Teide National Park, and Spain's tallest mountain at 3,717m (12,200ft). Particularly beautiful in May-June when the wild flowers are in bloom, the park's spectacular scenery makes for great hiking. There is a visitors' centre with details of walking trails, including one to the top of Mount Teide. You can take the cable car (*teleférico*) to within 160m (500ft) of the summit (long queues in summer).

collection of exotic flowers, trees, shrubs and cacti.

Above Puerto de la Cruz, the well-preserved town of **La Orotava**, with its collection of stately mansions, ancient churches and cobbled streets, is dominated by the Byzantine dome of the **Iglesia Nuestra Señor de la Concepción**.

Gran Canaria

Almost circular in shape, Gran Canaria is small enough to explore within a week, yet it has been described as a continent in miniature. The coastline ranges from awesome cliffs to golden dunes. Inland, you can choose between stark mountains and tranquil valleys. It is also well-supplied with beaches, shopping and sophisticated nightlife.

Bustling **Las Palmas** is a major commercial centre, cosmopolitan resort and seaport all in one. The heart of the city is **Santa Catalina Park**: one gigantic outdoor café, which buzzes night and day. The 3km (2-mile) sandy beach, **Playa de las Canteras**, is protected by an offshore reef.

Though often lumped under the collective title of Maspalomas, each of the three smart, new south-coast resorts has its own distinct characteristics: **San Agustin** is quiet and tidy; **Playa del Inglés** is more robust with plenty of fun-and-sun package tour hotels, plus some 50 discos at the last count; while **Maspalomas** is famous for its dunes, which are sufficiently large and unspoiled to constitute a sort of mini-Sahara.

Palmito Park, situated in a picturesque gorge some 13km (8 miles) to the north of Maspalomas, provides an excellent family day out. There are a variety of colourful caged birds

in the beautiful gardens – parrots and exotic free-flying residents, including toucans.

The mountainous heart of Gran Canaria makes for tiring driving, but wonderful **views** as you clamber up through the almond groves and thick pine forests. The most popular vantage point is **Cruz de Tejeda**, at 1,463m (4,800ft). Here, the panorama includes two rock formations. The most distinctive is the statuesque **Roque Nublo** (1,817m/5,961ft) and the other is Roque Betaiga. Both were once worshipped by the Guanches, the original inhabitants of the Canaries who migrated from North Africa.

Lanzarote

A later arrival on the tourist scene than either Gran Canaria or Tenerife, Lanzarote's development has been more controlled. It is a startling island,

Catch of the day: fresh fish and seafood feature prominently on local menus.

pock-marked with over 300 volcanoes. Still, the locals manage to grow onions, tomatoes, potatoes, melons and grapes, which spring in abundance from the volcanic ash.

The island's main resort is **Puerto del Carmen**. Its long, golden beach stretches for several kilometres and comfortably accommodates visitors. The **Costa Teguise**, just to the north of Arrecife (Lanzarote's undistinguished capital), offers modern holiday accommodation and several good beaches. The **Playa Cucheras** is notable for watersports.

Follow the east-coast road north to Guatiza, where prickly pears abound. The beautiful **Jardín de Cactus** here was designed by César Manrique. And there is more Manrique magic at the caves of **Jameos del Agua**, where a short fantasy journey through a landscaped grotto and underground lagoon takes you to a South Seas paradise!

The highlight of a trip to Lanzarote is a visit to the **Montañas de Fuego** (Mountains of Fire) in the Timanfaya

National Park. The stark, but scenically magnificent park starts just north of Yaiza. Its bizarre landscape of lava flows and rust-red mountains was largely formed over 16 months of cataclysmic volcanic activity during 1730-1.

Just inside the volcanic *malpaís* (badlands) of the park, you can take a **camel ride** up the slope of the volcanic cone. There is an information centre and car park at Islote de Hilario. Coach tours of 50 minutes depart from here every hour to explore the incredible lunar landscape.

Fuerteventura

Situated less than 100km (60 miles) off the coast of North Africa, Fuerteventura is a beach bum's paradise courtesy of the Sahara. There are miles of golden sandy beach, and the winds which originally blew the sand here still ensure superb windsurfing. Watersports aside, there is little else to do on this arid, treeless island.

Inland **Betancuria** is an attractive oasis. Fuerteventura's **127** first capital, it boasts the splendid 17th-century church of **Santa María**.

At the southern tip of the island, the **Jandía peninsula** offers terrific beaches, the best of which are on the less-developed **Costa Calma**. The Playa de Sotavento is a world-famous windsurfing area, and has terrific dunes.

La Gomera

A short boat trip to the south of Tenerife, Gomera remains an unspoiled island of steep, green terraced hills and tranquil valleys. Boats and hydrofoils dock at **San Sebastián**, the chief town, notable for its connections with Christopher Columbus, including a local church where he prayed and the house where he supposedly stayed in 1492.

A delight for walkers, the **Garajonay National Park** is

a World Heritage site, and home to the Alto de Garajonay, Gomera's highest peak (1,487m/4,878ft). The island's one and only beach resort is in the south, at the low-key **Playa de Santiago**.

La Palma

The most northwesterly of the Canaries, La Palma is lush and green. **Santa Cruz de la Palma**, the capital, is an appealing small town. There are two routes to choose from: a

*E*scaping the crowds is no problem on Fuerteventura's white sandy beaches.

northern loop, which culminates at the world-renowned Palma observatory (closed to the public) on top of the **Roque de los Muchachos**, the highest peak in Palma (2,423m/7,950ft). The highly recommended southern loop takes you to the magnificent **Caldera de Taburiente**. This giant crater has a circumference of some 27km (17 miles) and drops around 700m (2,300ft) into a fertile valley. It is perfect walking country with some marvellous views.

El Hierro

Until the voyages of Columbus, El Hierro was considered the end of the world, and little seems to have changed since. Few visitors arrive on the daily flight from Tenerife and tourist facilities are limited. **Valverde** is the tiny, quiet capital.

The **Mirador de la Peña**, 8km (5 miles) west of the airport, has fine views and a good restaurant. There's a stretch of coast too, **El Golfo**, part of a partially submerged volcano.

What to Do

Spain isn't just for seeing, it's also for doing. Whatever you get up to, whether it's bargaining in Madrid's *Rastro* market, betting on a *jai-alai* game in the Basque Country or dancing the *sardaña* in Barcelona, you will be absorbing the vitality and passion of the people, their pastimes and their rich, colourful culture.

Sports

With its seas and mountains, Spain offers every kind of sporting and leisure opportunity, as strenuous or relaxing as you choose, summer or winter. In Andalusia you can even ski in the mountains and swim in the sea on the same day.

On the Beach

Spain boasts hundreds of miles of sandy beaches, and pebbled and rocky shores too, excellent for snorkelling. As can be expected, the best beaches are often the most developed and offer a full range of facilities: watersports, parasols, deck-chairs, changing rooms, showers, bars, restaurants and cafés.

With a little enterprise you can still discover near-deserted coves, or head off to the less developed coasts such as the Costa de Almería or Costa de la Luz (see p.113).

Windsurfing. This is a hugely popular sport. Tuition, windsurfers and maybe wetsuit hire are available at most good resorts. Advanced windsurfers should go to Tarifa, southern Spain (see p.113), or Jandía peninsula on Fuerteventura (Canary Islands).

Waterskiing. An expensive pursuit these days, waterskiing is still available at large resorts – as are jet-skiing and parascending. The Balearics, and east-coast resorts at La Manga,

*C*atamarans for hire on the beach; fishing is popular along the rocky shoreline.

the Costa Dorada and Costa Brava are all good places to try this exhilarating sport.

Scuba diving. There is good diving off the Costa Brava, Costa de Almería and Balearic Islands. Local dive operators can arrange tuition, permits and equipment hire.

Boating. Most tourist beaches have a variety of craft for hire – light catamarans are very popular. Sailing is particularly good off the Costa Brava, the

Balearic and Canary Islands, in the Bay of Cádiz and at Santander and Laredo on Spain's north coast.

Sports Ashore

Golf. Spain is world famous for golf with over 100 courses on the mainland and islands. Not every pro is a Seve Ballesteros, but the quality of instruction, should you want it is generally high. The greatest concentration is on the Costa del Sol with 24 courses. On the east coast, the Valencian courses of *El Saler* and *El Escorpian* are highly rated and good value; the *La Manga Club* on the Costa Cálida has three championship courses. Of the islands, Majorca has nine courses; while Gran Canaria boasts Spain's oldest golf club, in a stunning setting.

For an overview of what's available, request a golfing map of Spain from the national tourist office.

Tennis. Tennis is another favourite sport in Spain but, unless you know you will be able to play under floodlights, it may be best to avoid playing in the hottest months of the

Jai-Alai – The World's Fastest Ball Game

The ancient Basque game of *jai-alai* (pronounced 'high-a-lie', but sometimes known as *pelota*) is played throughout the Basque region.

Every town and almost every village, no matter how tiny, has a *frontón*, or pitch, rather like a squash court, where the players hurl themselves around after the *pelota* (ball) which is propelled at the back wall at speeds of up to 303kph (188mph) by woven straw scoops attached to the players' hands.

The basic rules are similar to tennis or squash – the ball may only bounce once on the ground; each game comprises 7-9 points. Far more complex is the betting, which is largely incomprehensible to outsiders.

year. Many hotels, apartment and villa complexes have their own tennis courts and perhaps a resident professional. The Costa del Sol is probably the biggest centre for tennis tuition; and the east coast *La Manga Club* is one of the best tennis centres in Europe.

Horse Riding. There are ranches and equestrian centres all over Spain. Many offer tuition and a range of outings from a gentle seaside trot to a stimulating cross-country excursion, or overnight treks.

Skiing. Spain's 27 ski resorts are attracting an increasing number of devotees. Over half of these are in the Pyrenees (including Andorra), with another four resorts in the Picos de Europa. Europe's sunniest skiing takes place in the Andalusian Sierra Nevada.

Walking, Hiking and Climbing. Spain offers numerous opportunities for the outdoor type in a network of national parks and nature reserves. There are two mountain parks

A natural climbing wall at Mijas, Andalusia, in the foothills of the Serranía de Ronda.

in the Pyrenees and another in the Picos de Europa, with walking trails, hiking paths and climbing for enthusiasts of all abilities. Other favourite outdoor centres include the dunes and wetlands of the Doñana National Park in the southwest, and the volcanic badlands of Tenerife.

133

Shopping

Modern Spain has long since shed its image as the bargain basement of Europe. However, fans of the truly kitsch should have no fear, for amongst the genuinely tasteful souvenirs of a Spanish holiday – ceramics, leather goods, food treats from olive oil to nougat – the straw donkey and bullfight poster are still alive and kicking.

For a quick survey of what Spaniards are buying, browse through the big department stores: *El Corte Inglés* and the *Galerías Preciados*. There are branches of both stores in most sizeable towns. Unlike the majority of Spanish businesses, these chains stay open non-stop across the lunch-and-siesta break until around 8pm in the evening. For the quality crafts, more than a dozen cities have branches of *Artespaña*, the official showcase for items created by Spanish artisans.

Here are a few suggestions for best buys in Spain:

Antiques. You will find few bargains in genuine antique shops or stalls but the open-air bric-à-brac markets, such as Madrid's *Rastro*, provide plenty of fun for browsers.

Artificial pearls. Made in Majorca, these are so convincing often experts are fooled – until they feel them. Rub them

There are pottery bargains galore in Spanish markets, so shop around for the best prices.

along your teeth – the real ones are rougher.

Ceramics. Each region produces its own distinctive designs and colour schemes. Handpainted *azulejos* (tiles of Moorish origins) are also a popular collectable.

Damascene and Toledo steel. This is a speciality of Toledo, though the art of damascene (inlaying the steel with intricate gold designs) originated in Damascus.

Embroidery and lace. Pretty embroidered linen and traditional lacework is sold all over Spain. Look for lace *mantillas*, those lightweight shawls used for covering shoulders. However, be wary of gypsy street sellers offering bargain prices; their goods are generally of much poorer quality and made anywhere but in Spain.

Glassware. Majorca is the centre for glassmaking. The typical blue, green or amber bowls, glasses and pitchers are sold in many mainland stores.

*P*eerless artificial pearls from the island of Majorca can fool even the experts.

Leather. Top quality Spanish-leather products ranging from sturdy belts, wallets and riding boots to elegant handbags and jackets are an excellent buy.

Valencian porcelain. Lladró figurine collectors can stock up at the company's Madrid showroom (Calle de Quintana 2); less detailed models from the same workshop go under the name *Nao*.

135

Entertainment

Whether its a local *fiesta* or a grand Easter parade, a cousin's wedding or a night out on the town, the Spanish love a good party. The challenge here is to keep to the pace, or to change your own routine to get on an even footing.

Nightlife

Since Spaniards don't usually start thinking about their dinner until 9 or 10pm, Spanish nightlife tends to keep going far later than in other countries. After a leisurely meal, it's on to the **music bar** (occasionally live music, but generally a video screen pumping up the volume), for a drink and a chance to catch the latest football score before deciding where to go next. Only then, will they actually hit the **disco** or **nightclub** – around 2am. Currently, Barcelona is one of the most fashionable nightspots in Europe. Madrid is the city that never sleeps and Ibiza is the leader of the pack in the Mediterranean.

Flamenco

Throbbing guitars, snapping fingers, stamping heels and soul-stirring songs lure local enthusiasts and visitors to Spain's flamenco nightclubs. There are two main groups of songs: the bouncier, more cheerful type is known as *cante chico*; the *cante jonto* deals with love, death and human drama in slow, piercing style. The purists have little time for the show-biz style *tabloas flamenco* (floorshows) of Madrid and the resorts. For the real thing you have to head for the specialist bars and clubs of Andalusia, the home of flamenco.

Bullfighting

To the Spanish, the bullfight (*corrida)* is neither a sport nor a contest between two equals. It's about the ritualistic slaughter of the bull, and each stage of a bullfight is clearly laid out and understood by the crowd.

First, the *matador* gets the measure of the bull with the aid of his large red and yellow *capote* (cape). Then the *picadores* (mounted spearmen) arrive and attempt to lance the bull's neck muscles in order to lower the head and make the *matador*'s kill easier. The *banerilleros*, on foot, then plant long, coloured darts into the hump on the bull's neck. Finally, the *matador* returns and taunts the bull with the small, dark red *muleta* cape. When the *matador* thinks he has achieved domination and the moment is right, he delivers his *coup de grâce* – in theory, a single, swift sword stroke over the bull's horns and down between the shoulder blades into the heart. In practice, it often takes more than one attempt.

The season for the *corrida* lasts from March to October.

Cultural Activities

Spaniards take **opera** very seriously, along with their home-grown stars Plácido Domingo, José Carreras, Teresa Berganza and Monserrat Caballé. There are three great venues: Barcelona's Gran Teatre del Liceu; Madrid's Teatro Real; and Seville's new Teatro de la Maestranza.

For **concerts**, Madrid's new Auditorio Nacional de Música

*A*t fiesta time, Spanish dancers take to the streets in their regional costume.

Folklore and Festivals

Neither the Las Vegas-style flamenco cabarets staged in major resorts nor that perennial favourite of package-tour operators, the 'folkloric evening' (mediocre food, industrial-strength red wine and a spot of lacklustre castanet clicking) is the ideal introduction to Spanish culture.

The best way to experience Spanish customs and traditions at work (and play) is to join the fiesta, catch up with a carnival, and seek out a genuine flamenco club. Check with the tourist office for details of local celebrations during your stay. Here's a selection of the very best from around the country:

February/March: *Carnival*, processions in Santa Cruz de Tenerife, Cádiz and Sitges.

March/April: *Semana Santa* (Holy Week), processions in all major cities.

April: *April Fair*, parades, dancing and bullfights in Seville.

May: *Festival of the Patios and International Flamenco Festival*, Seville. *Horse Fair*, Jerez de la Frontera.

May/June: *Fiesta de San Isidro*, bullfighting, concerts and fun fairs in Madrid.

June: *Corpus Christi*, festivities in Granada, Toledo, Sitges and the Canary Islands. *Flamenco Festival*, Badajoz.

July: *Fiesta de San Fermín*, bullruns, bullfights and festivities in Pamplona. *Music Festival*, Granada. *Guitar Festival*, Seville. *Festival of St James*, Santiago de Compostela.

August: *Assumption*, traditional commemoration in La Alberca (Salamanca). *Summer Fair*, Málaga.

September: *Logroño Wine Harvest*, festival in Jerez de la Frontera, *Feria de San Miguel*, Torremolinos. *Meced Festival*, music and folklore in Barcelona.

138 **October**: *Pilar Festival*, processions and folklore in Zaragoza.

is home to the Spanish National Orchestra. Check with local tourist offices for details of concerts and recitals in other cities. They often take place in historic surroundings such as churches and palaces.

For **drama**, Spanish as well as foreign plays – classical and contemporary – can be seen in theatres all over the country.

Foreign films are generally dubbed before they are shown in a Spanish **cinema** but in major cities and some resorts, cinemas may show films in their original version (labelled 'v.o.') with Spanish subtitles.

Children

Long, sunny days and soft, sandy beaches mean that much of coastal Spain is a favourite family destination. Many hotels have special features for junior guests, ranging from organized poolside games and outings to babysitting facilities. When the appeal of seawater and sandcastles starts to wear thin, you can always try some of the following:

Make a splash. Water parks are a highly popular alternative to a day at the beach. While the energetic kids hurl themselves down waterslides and ride the machine-made waves, the less active types can top up their tans in landscaped gardens. Additional attractions often include ten-pin bowling and mini-golf .

Go-karting. A favourite with the kids (not to mention their parents), go-kart tracks are common along the *costas*.

A night out. The Spanish take their kids out at night, so why not do likewise? Older children will probably enjoy a colourful flamenco show, and there are few restrictions, if any, on children accompanying adults into bars, restaurants or cafés.

Fiesta. Older children will love the firework displays and music, while the younger kids watch the dancers and giant papier-mâché figures wide-eyed. Carnival is always a colourful event where the local **139**

A bird's eye view from the big wheel at Tibidabo, perched high above Barcelona.

children usually wear the best costumes. There is nothing to stop you also dressing up and joining in. It's great fun and you're sure to be welcome.

The Fun of the Fair. Most big towns or resorts have a *parque de atracciones* where the rides range from the old-fashioned carousel and big-wheel to high-tech thrills. Barcelona's two fun fairs, Montjuïc and Tibidabo, deserve a special mention for their first-class rides and tremendous views.

Animal life. The Barcelona Zoo, with its famous albino gorilla and a killer whale and dolphin show, is acclaimed as one of the finest zoo parks in Europe. Elsewhere on the *costas*, marine parks with performing dolphins, sealions and other animal shows are becoming increasingly popular.

140

Eating Out

The Spanish take their food very seriously and you will rarely be disappointed by the choice, the tasty flavour or the hearty portions served in local restaurants throughout Spain. Each region has its distinct culinary strengths, from the seafood creations of the north to the rice platters of the east, from the roasts of the central area to the succulent hams and fried fish of the south. And for every dish there is usually a locally grown wine to match.

WHERE TO EAT

Spanish restaurants are graded by the 'fork' system. One fork is the lowest grade, five forks is the élite. These ratings, however, are awarded according to the facilities and degree of luxury that the restaurant can offer, not for the quality of the food. (See RECOMMENDED RESTAURANTS p.182).

If you are in search of the type of restaurant which specializes in local food rather than fancy napkins, look out for the word *típica*. For good value, all Spanish restaurants should offer a *menú del día* (daily special). This is normally a three-course meal, including house wine, at a very reasonable set price.

The prices on the menu include a service charge and taxes, but it's customary to leave a tip of 5-10 per cent if you've been served efficiently. Bars and cafés, like restaurants, usually include a service

*A*lthough prices have increased with the quality of food, you can still find cheap eateries. **141**

charge, but additional small tips are customary. Prices are 10-15 per cent lower if you stand or sit at the bar rather than occupy a table.

Two notes of caution: the prices of *tapas*, those tasty bar snacks, are not always indicated and can be surprisingly expensive – so do ask before ordering. Also ask how much your bill will be when ordering fish or seafood, which is priced by the 100g weight.

The price is based on the uncooked weight and can be very expensive.

Meal times are generally later in Spain than the rest of Europe. The peak hours are from 1 to 3.30pm for lunch and from 8.30 to 11pm for dinner. In some parts of the country (like Madrid) meals are taken very late, only starting at around 10pm. However, in tourist areas or big cities, you can get a meal at most places just about any time of day.

WHAT TO EAT

Breakfast

For Spaniards, this is the least significant meal of the day and will probably just consist of *tostado* (toast), or a roll and coffee. If you have a sweet tooth, *churros* are deep-fried and sugared temptations.

To make their guests feel at home, most hotels offer breakfast buffets with a selection of cereals, fresh and dried fruit, cold meats and cheeses, plus bacon and eggs.

Lunch and Dinner

The classic Spanish dish is *paella*, named after the black iron pan in which the saffron rice base is cooked in stock. The cook then adds various combinations of squid, *chorizo* (spicy sausage), chicken, mussels, prawns, shrimps, rabbit, onion, peppers, peas and so on, according to what is to hand or the type of *paella* advertised on the menu. It is always cooked to order (usually for a minimum of two people).

There are two other national favourites which are well known to visitors. The first is *gazpacho*, a delicious Andalusian chilled soup to which chopped tomatoes, peppers, cucumbers, onions and fried croutons are added. The second is *tortilla*, or potato omelette. There are many variations on this theme, served hot or cold.

Regional Tastes

Every province, and almost every town, in Spain seems to have its own locally produced

F or a snack or a meal, tapas is the business (above); stirring up a seafood sensation (left).

sausage, cheese, a variation on *paella* – and their own secret ingredients for *cocido* – a rich cold-weather meat and vegetable hot-pot. Here are a few suggestions for what's cooking around the country, moving roughly north to south.

Galicia: Great seafood; *caldo gallego* (a hearty vegetable soup); *empanada* (flaky pastry parcel stuffed with meat or seafood, served hot or cold).

Asturias: *Fabada asturiana* (big white bean and sausage casserole); *merluza a la sidra* (hake in cider sauce); *queso de Cabrales* (pungent, piquant, creamy blue cheese).

Basque Country: Seafood is king here: *bacalao al pil pil* (fried cod in hot garlic sauce); *chipirones* (tiny squid); *marmitako* (spicy tuna, tomato and potato stew).

The Pyrenees: Hearty, warming meat dishes in *chilindrón* sauce (tomatoes, peppers, garlic, ham and wine); game dishes and mountain trout.

Catalonia: *Esqueixada* salad (grilled or baked vegetables in olive oil); grilled fish with sauce *Romesco* (nuts, chili, tomatoes, garlic and breadcrumbs); seafood stews like *zarzuela* and *suquet de Peix*.

Castile: Try *sopa castellana* for starters (a baked garlic soup with chunks of ham and an egg poaching in it); *cochinillo asado* (suckling pig); *cordero asado* (roast lamb).

The East Coast: Valencia is the home of paella, also *arroz con costra* (rice with pork meatballs).

A temple of good taste: Spanish pastelerías are packed with epicurian delights.

La Mancha: Quixote country is famed for its game dishes; *tojunto* (rabbit stew); *pisto manchego* (an extravagant ratatouille-like vegetable stew with aubergines, tomatoes and courgettes); *queso manchego*, Spain's favourite cheese.

Extremadura: Country-style pork and lamb; countless varieties of sausage.

Andalusia: *Gazpacho* and *ajo blanco* (or *gazpacho blanco*, made from garlic and almonds garnished with grapes); *fritura mixta* or *pescaito frito* (pieces of fish fried in a light batter); *huevos a la flamenca* (egg, tomato and vegetable bake with chorizo, prawns, ham).

The Islands: Canarian specialities include *papas arrugadas* (new potatoes baked and rolled in rock salt) served with *mojo picón* (piquant red sauce); *mojo verde* (green herb sauce served with fish). On Majorca, sample *tumbet* (ratatouille and potato-type casserole with meat or fish).

Tapas

A *tapa* is a small portion of food which encourages you to keep drinking instead of heading off to a restaurant for a meal. Once upon a time, *tapas* were given away, but that is rare these days. However, bars which specialize in *tapas* are more popular than ever.

Bona-fide *tapas* bars, and indeed many others, have a whole counter display of hot and cold *tapas*, which makes choosing easy. Just point out one you like the look of – anything from olives, meatballs, local cheese, prawns in garlic, marinated anchovies or *chorizo* (spicy sausage) to meatballs or *tortilla* (wedges of Spanish omelette). On portion control: *una tapa* is the smallest amount; *una ración* is half a small plateful; and *una porción* is almost a meal in itself.

Sweet-tooth Specials

The ubiquitous Spanish dessert is *flan* (*crème caramel*). The Catalans do a deluxe version, *crema catalana*, which is flavoured with lemon and cinnamon, and many towns have their own recipes for *yemas*, a monumentally sweet egg-yolk and sugar confection.

Otherwise, you can head for the *pastelerías* (cake shops) for a vast repertoire of cakes, tarts and pastries. Marzipan

*F*rexinet is one of Spain's most prestigious producers of sparkling cava wines.

and *turrón* (nougat) also come in various guises with regional variations.

WHAT TO DRINK

Wines and Alcoholic Drinks

Spain has more square kilometres of vineyards than any other European country. Vintage pundits confidently compare the best Spanish wines with the most respected foreign classics, causing controversy in some global wine circles. On the other hand, much of the crop is plonk, intended for home consumption and never meant to grace the glasses of experts.

The better Spanish wines are regulated by the *Denominación de Origen* quality control. If a bottle is marked DOC, you can be sure the wine was made in a particular region and its producers followed the strictest rules.

Regarding table wine, the oldest and most vigorously protected *denominación* is

Rioja, and some truly distinguished reds (*tinto*) are grown along the Ebro valley in northern Spain. East of La Rioja, Aragon contributes some powerful Cariñena reds. The best-known wines from central Spain, the splendidly smooth reds of Valdepeñas, come from La Mancha.

The Penedès region of Catalonia is acclaimed not only for its excellent still wines, largely whites (*blanco*), but also for its *cava*, a sparkling wine made by the *methode champenoise*.

In the southwest, Jerez de la Frontera is the home of sherry. As an aperitif, try a chilled, dry *fino* or medium-dry *amontillado*. A dark, sweet *oloroso* goes down well after dinner.

Spain also produces several sweet dessert wines, such as *moscatel*. A good *moscatel*, from Málaga say, will taste of sultanas and honey.

Spanish brandy is often sweeter and heavier than French Cognac. It is a vital ingredient in *sangría*, probably the most popular tourist drink in Spain. It's a mixture of red wine, orange and lemon juice, brandy, mineral water, sugar, sliced fruit and ice.

Beer (*cerveza*) is generally fizzy and not very strong. There are plenty of Spanish brands, and foreign beers are widely available. A small beer is *una cerveza pequeña*; *una cerveza grande* is about the same size as a British pint.

Tea, Coffee and Soft Drinks

The Spanish usually drink coffee (*café*) as opposed to tea (*té*). This can be either *solo*, small and black; *con leche*, a large cup made with milk; or *cortado*, a tiny cup with a little milk. Spanish coffee is nearly always strong. If you prefer it weaker, ask for *nescafé*.

Mineral water (*agua mineral*) is either sparkling (*con gas*) or still (*sin gas*). Ice-cream parlours (*heladería*) sell *granizado*, slushy iced fruit juices, and fresh orange juice (*zumo de naranjas*), though the latter can be surprisingly expensive considering oranges are one of Spain's main crops. **147**

To Help You Order...

Could we have a table? **¿Nos puede dar una mesa?**
Do you have a set menu? **¿Tiene un menú del día?**
I'd like a/an/some… **Quisiera…**

beer	**una cerveza**	milk	**leche**
bread	**pan**	mineral water	**agua mineral**
coffee	**un café**	potatoes	**patatas**
dessert	**un postre**	rice	**arroz**
fish	**pescado**	salad	**una ensalada**
fruit	**fruta**	sandwich	**un bocadillo**
glass	**un vaso**	sugar	**azúcar**
ice-cream	**un helado**	tea	**un té**
meat	**carne**	water (iced)	**agua (fresca)**
menu	**la carta**	wine	**vino**

and Read the Menu...

aceitunas	olives	**langosta**	spiny lobster
albóndigas	meat balls	**langostino**	large prawn
almejas	baby clams	**lomo**	loin
atún	tunny (tuna)	**mariscos**	shellfish
bacalao	codfish	**mejillones**	mussels
besugo	sea bream	**melocotón**	peach
boquerones	fresh anchovies	**merluza**	hake
calamares	squid	**ostras**	oysters
callos	tripe	**pastel**	cake
caracoles	snails	**pollo**	chicken
cerdo	pork	**pulpitos**	baby octopus
chuleta	chops	**salsa**	sauce
cocido	stew	**ternera**	veal
cordero	lamb	**tortilla**	omelet
entremeses	hors-d'oeuvre	**trucha**	trout
gambas	prawns	**uvas**	grapes

BLUEPRINT
for a
Perfect Trip

An A–Z Summary of Practical Information

> Listed after most main entries is an appropriate Spanish translation, usually in the singular. You'll find this vocabulary useful when asking for information or assistance.

A

ACCOMMODATION (See Camping on p.151, Youth Hostels on p.172, and the list of Recommended Hotels on p.174)

All hotels in Spain are government inspected and graded 1-5 stars upon facilities. The majority of tourist accommodation in Spain is provided by 3- or 4-star hotels which conform to reasonable international standards. Apartments and aparthotels may be found in more popular coastal resorts.

Hostales, modest hotels with few facilities, denoted by the sign '*Hs*', and *pensiones* (pensions), boarding houses denoted by the letter '*P*', are graded 1-3 stars. The most basic forms of accommodation are the *casas de huéspedes* ('*CH*') and *fondas* ('*F*').

The letter '*R*', suffixed to a hotel or hostel sign, indicates *residencia*. In theory, this means that there is no restaurant and the establishment offers bed-and-breakfast only, but this is not always the case.

Spain's most notable accommodation is usually found in *paradores*. These are state-run establishments, sometimes set in historic buildings, or sometimes in modern blocks in outstanding surroundings. Their aim is to provide the chance to experience 'the real Spain'. The central reservation agency for *paradores* is Paradores de España, Central de Reservas, Velázquez 18, 28001 Madrid (tel. 435 97 00, fax 435 99 44).

When booking into any kind of accommodation, you will be asked to surrender your passport for a short period. In general, prices are quoted per room (as opposed to per person). Value added tax (IVA) of 6 per cent is added to the bill, or 15 per cent at 5-star hotels. Hotels in the Canary Islands charge 4 per cent IVA regardless of category.

a single/double room	**una habitación individual/doble**
with bath/shower	**con baño/ducha**
What's the rate per night?	**¿Cuál es el precio por noche?**

AIRPORTS (aeropuerto) (See also TRAVELLING TO SPAIN on p.170)

Madrid's Barajas aiport (14km/9 miles east of the capital) is Spain's main air transport hub, with frequent connections to regional airports throughout the country.

There are also international airports at Barcelona, Bilbao, Oviedo, Santiago de Compostela, Seville, Valencia and Zaragoza. With Spain's domestic airline, Aviaco, it is possible to fly to another 21 airports. If you intend to use internal flights, ask about discount air-passes such as the 'freedom of the Spanish airways' pass from Iberia, Spain's national carrier.

C

CAMPING (camping)

Spanish campgrounds are divided into four categories (luxury, 1st, 2nd and 3rd class), and rates and facilities vary accordingly. All sites, however, have drinking water, toilets and showers, electricity, basic first-aid facilities, safes for valuables and all are under surveillance night and day. Ask the national tourist office to send you their free map detailing campsites.

We have a tent/caravan (trailer).	**Tenemos una tienda de camping/una caravana.**

CAR HIRE/RENTAL (coches de alquilar) (See also DRIVING on p.156)

You will find local and international car hire firms all over Spain offering a wide range of cars at varying prices.

Third-party insurance is included in the basic hire charge, and usually CDW (Collision Damage Waiver). Personal accident insurance is normally covered by your standard travel insurance policy.

You must be over 21 if you are paying by credit card and over 23 if you are paying by cash. In the latter case, a large additional deposit may be required. Although officially you should have an International Driving Permit or a recent EU driving licence with translations supplied, in practice, driving licences from all major countries are accepted without question.

CLIMATE and CLOTHING

As a general rule, late spring to early summer and late summer to early autumn are the best times for visiting most parts of Spain. This avoids the most oppressive heat, not to mention the crowds and high season accommodation rates. In winter, temperatures in the high central-plains region plummet.

Summer temperatures in the north are ideal for swimming and sunning, but expect rain any time in the northwest. At the height of summer (July-August) even the locals try to escape the dry, merciless heat of Madrid and the central plains; while the southern and east coast areas can be uncomfortably humid.

For winter sun, head for the Canary Islands where temperatures rarely fall below a monthly average of 17°C (62°F). On the mainland, the south coast and parts of the central and southern east coast are pleasantly mild year-round, but swimming is not really an option. Of course, winter is the best time for skiing in the Pyrenees, Picos de Europa and Andalusia's Sierra Nevada.

Clothing. If you're heading for the south coast in the height of summer, pack loose cotton clothes and remember sun hats and sun care lotion. In April, May and October, you may need a light pullover for

the evenings. From November to March, you can enjoy shirt-sleeve sunshine during the day, but this can be interrupted by chill winds from the mountains.

Winter visitors to Madrid and the central plains region will need to pack warm clothing. If you're heading for the northwest at any time, take waterproof gear.

Dress codes are very casual in most resorts, but tourists sporting resortwear in a big, sophisticated city like Madrid or Barcelona may attract stares.

The Spanish enjoy dressing up for an occasion, and it is as well to look smart if you are visiting a good restaurant or reputable night-club. Micro, tattered shorts and beachwear are considered inappropriate attire for visits to churches.

A word of warning: make sure you pack all you need in the way of changes of clothes. Hotel laundry bills are astronomical.

COMMUNICATIONS

Post Offices (*correos*). Post offices handle mail and telegrams only; normally you cannot make telephone calls from them. Hours vary slightly from town to town, but routine postal services are generally from 8am to noon and 5-7.30pm, Monday-Friday, and mornings only on Saturday.

There is generally only one post office per town, and it is usually very busy. Fortunately, postage stamps (*sellos*) are also on sale at tobacconists (*tabacos*), at hotel desks and at tourist shops selling postcards. Mail for destinations outside Spain should be posted in the box marked *extranjeros* (overseas).

If you don't know where you'll be staying in advance, you can have mail forwarded to you at a convenient post office. Envelopes should be addressed *Lista de Correos* (poste restante) with the name of the town. When collecting mail, take your passport along as identification.

Telephones (*teléfono*). The Spanish national telephone company, Teléfonica, has telephone centres in most large towns where you can make cash, credit card or collect/reverse charge (*cobro revertido*) calls. Both local and international direct-dial calls can be made from phone boxes which accept 5, 25 and 100 pta coins, and phone cards (*tarjeta telefónica*), which can be bought from post offices and *tabacos*. The latter are advisable for international calls.

To make an international call, pick up the receiver, wait for the dial tone, then dial 07; wait for the second tone, then dial the country code (44 for the UK, 1 for the US and Canada), the area code (minus the first 0), and the subscriber number.

If you are tempted to call home from your hotel, check the price of a three-minute call before you dial. Hotels often add a surcharge of as much as 30 per cent on top of the actual cost of the call.

When making a call within Spain, but outside the region, add 9 at the beginning of the area code, i.e. the area code for Madrid is 1, but you will need to dial 91; Barcelona would be 93; Seville 95; Valencia 96. The 9 prefix should be dropped if you are dialling from outside Spain. Spain's country code is 34.

COMPLAINTS

By law, all hotels and restaurants must keep official complaints forms (*Hojas de Reclamación*) and produce one on demand. The original of this triplicate document should be sent to the regional tourist office of the Ministry of Tourism, one copy remains with the establishment, and you keep the third sheet. Merely asking for a complaint form is usually enough to resolve any problems, since tourism authorities take a serious view of complaints and your host wants to keep both his reputation and his licence intact. If you fail to obtain satisfaction from the manager, take your complaint to the local tourist office (see TOURIST INFORMATION OFFICES, p.168).

CRIME

The most common crime against the tourist in Spain is theft from hire cars. If you park overnight in the street in one of the big towns or resorts, there is every chance your car will be broken into. Always look for secure parking areas.

Thieves also operate at tourist locations where cars are left unattended. Never leave anything of value in your car at any time. Hotels
recommend that you use the safe deposit box in your room – for

which there is usually a charge – for all valuables, including your passport. Burglaries at holiday apartments do occur, so keep doors and windows locked when you are out and while you are asleep.

Beware of pickpockets, particularly in crowded places such as markets, bus or subway stations, discos and fiesta-type street parties. You should report all thefts to the local police within 24 hours for your own insurance purposes.

On a more cheerful note, crimes involving violence against tourists are rare.

I want to report a theft. **Quiero denunciar un robo.**

CUSTOMS (aduna) and ENTRY FORMALITIES

Most visitors, including citizens of all EU countries, the US, Canada, Eire, Australia and New Zealand, require only a valid passport – no visa or health certificate – to enter Spain. Visitors from South Africa must have a visa.

If you plan to stay for more than 90 days (US citizens 180 days), a Spanish consulate or tourist office can advise you before you leave.

Duty-Free. As Spain is part of the EU, free exchange of non-duty free goods for personal use is permitted between Spain and the UK and the Republic of Ireland. However, duty free items are still subject to restrictions: check before you go. For residents of non-EU countries, restrictions are as follows: **Australia**: 250 cigarettes or 250g tobacco; 1l alcohol; **Canada**: 200 cigarettes and 50 cigars and 400g tobacco; 1.1l spirits or wine or 8.5l beer; **New Zealand**: 200 cigarettes or 50 cigars or 250g tobacco; 4.5l wine or beer and 1.1l spirits; **South Africa**: 400 cigarettes and 50 cigars and 250g tobacco; 2l wine and 1l spirits; **USA**: 200 cigarettes and 100 cigars or a 'reasonable amount' of tobacco.

Tourists may bring an unlimited amount of Spanish or foreign currency into Spain and take out (undeclared) up to the equivalent of 1 million pesetas.

I've nothing to declare. **No tengo nada que declarar.**

It's for my own personal use. **Es para mi uso personal.**

D

DRIVING

Arrival. If you want to bring your own car to Spain, you will need the car registration papers, a nationality plate or sticker, a red warning triangle, a Green Card extension to your regular insurance policy, and a bail bond which can also be arranged through your insurance company. Drivers who do not have a pink EU-type driving licence will need an International Driving Permit or translation of their current licence.

Driving conditions. Similar to other countries on the continent, you must drive on the right, overtake on the left, and yield right of way to all vehicles coming from your right.

Main roads are very good, and even country roads are generally well surfaced. The *autopista* (motorway or freeway) is usually the fastest way to get about but it does not allow you to see much of the country, and the tolls (*peaje*) can be high.

Beware of driving anywhere on a Sunday evening. Massive traffic jams are likely to build up, both on and off the *autopista*, as city weekenders head back from the beach or country.

Driving and parking is a nightmare in large Spanish cities, and not much better in many towns. If you are planning a city-based holiday, think again about hiring a car. Look into public transport options or tours for day trips to attractions beyond the city limits (see GUIDES AND TOURS on p.160).

Parking. Metered parking is common in both large and small towns, and your car will be towed away if you park illegally. It is an offence to park a car facing against the traffic.

Traffic police. Armed civil guards (*Guardia Civil*) patrol the roads. In towns, the municipal police handle traffic control. If you are fined for a traffic offence, you will have to pay on the spot.

Rules and Regulations. Always carry your driving licence and/or
International Driving Permit with you. The police can also demand

to see your passport at any time, so it is a good idea to carry a photocopy of the important pages. Spanish law requires that your car should carry two red warning triangles, and a set of spare headlamp and rearlamp bulbs. Seatbelts are compulsory when driving outside built-up city areas. Children under ten must travel in the rear.

Motorcyclists and pillion riders must wear crash helmets; and motorcycle lights must always be switched on.

Speed limits are set at 120kph on motorways; 100kph on dual carriageways or overtaking lanes; 90kph (70kph for vehicles with trailers) on other roads outside built-up areas; and 50kph or less within built-up areas.

driving licence	**carné de conducir**
car registration papers	**permiso de circulación**
Green Card	**carta verde**
Can I park here?	**¿Se puede aparcar aqui?**
Are we on the right road for...?	**¿Es ésta la carretera hacia…?**
Fill the tank please.	**Llénelo, por favor.**
Check the oil/tyres/battery.	**Por favor, controle el aceite/ los neumáticos/la batería.**
I've broken down.	**Mi coche se ha estropeado.**
There's been an accident.	**Ha habido un accidente.**
Can you send a mechanic?	**¿Puede usted mandar un mecánico?**

Distance

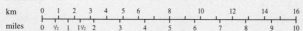

Fluid measures

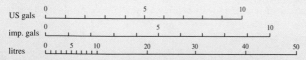

ELECTRIC CURRENT (*corriente elétrica*)

A 220-volt current is the norm, though if you are in an old building in the countryside, you may find a 125-volt current. If in doubt, ask.

If you have trouble with an appliance, ask your hotel receptionist or courier to recommend an *electricista*.

EMBASSIES and CONSULATES (*embajadas y consulados*)

All embassies (a selection of which are listed below) are in Madrid, and many countries have consular facilities in large cities such as Barcelona and Seville, as well as in resort areas popular with foreign tourists such as the Costa del Sol and Palma, the capital of Majorca. If you run into trouble with the authorities or the police, the embassy can advise you where to find the nearest consulate.

Australia: Paseo de la Castellana 143; tel. 279 85 04

Canada: Núñez de Balboa 35; tel. 431 43 00

Eire: Claudio Coello 73; tel. 576 35 09

South Africa: Claudio Coello 91; tel. 435 66 88

UK: Fernando el Santo 16; tel. 319 02 08. *Consulate*: Marqués de la Ensenada 16; tel. 308 52 01

US: Serrano 75; tel. 577 40 00

EMERGENCIES (*urgencia*) (See MEDICAL CARE on p.162, and POLICE on p.166)

If your hotel receptionist or courier isn't on hand to help and you have a real crisis, dial the **police emergency** number **091**.

ENVIRONMENTAL ISSUES

You may be tempted to buy exotic souvenirs for you and your family on your holiday, but spare a thought for endangered plants and animals which may be threatened by your purchase. Even trade in tourist souvenirs can threaten the most endangered species.

Over 800 species of animals and plants are currently banned from international trade by CITES (Convention on International Trade in Endangered Species and Plants). These include many corals, shells, cacti, orchids and hardwoods, as well as the more obvious tigers, rhinos, spotted cats and turtles.

So think twice before you buy – it may be illegal and your souvenirs could be confiscated by Customs on your return.

For further information or a factsheet, contact the following:

UK – Department of the Environment; tel. 01179 878961 (birds, reptiles and fish), or 01179 878168 (plants and mammals).

US – Fish and Wildlife Service; tel. (001) 703 358 2095; fax (001) 703 358 2281.

ETIQUETTE

The Spanish are still, by and large, an easy-going, friendly people – though you may not think so caught in a Madrid traffic jam or battling through rush-hour on the Barcelona subway. But then, the *madrileños* and the Catalans are something of a law unto themselves – more dynamic and more European than many of their compatriots, but no less friendly.

Most Spaniards still share a belief in the virtues of *mañana*: never do today what you can put off until tomorrow. There is no point in trying to rush them either. Far from making things better, it might lengthen the delay. Dealings in the bank or the post office can take an inordinate amount of time as pleasantries are exchanged and grandchildren solicitously asked after, but that is the Spanish way and you are not going to change it.

Politeness and simple courtesies do still matter here. Always begin a conversation with *buenos días* (good morning) or *buenas tardes* (good afternoon) and sign off with *adiós* (goodbye) or *buenas noches* (goodnight) when leaving. A handshake never goes amiss. One of the most enjoyable features of Spanish everyday life is the evening *paseo* when young and old alike come out to stroll around, see and be seen, and build up an appetite for supper.

When eating in a restaurant you must always ask for the bill. It is very rarely offered as no waiter wishes to be seen to be actually encouraging you to leave. Since a service charge is normally included in hotel and restaurant bills, tipping is not obligatory – but if the service was good, you might leave around 10 per cent of the bill.

When sightseeing, dress respectfully for visits to churches. And don't forget the sacred Spanish siesta when planning your itinerary. Many museums and attractions, as well as shops and businesses, are firmly closed from around 1 or 2pm until 4 or 5pm.

Children are welcome just about wherever you go in Spain from the bar to the bullring, and they'll enjoy the fuss that's made of them. And on the subject of bullrings, whatever you may think of bullfighting, if you attend a *corrida* never, never cheer the bull. It is considered an insult to the *matador*, to tradition and, by association, to the entire crowd. (See also Bullfighting on p.136.)

G

GUIDES and TOURS

An English-speaking guide can be contacted through most local tourist offices. Tourist offices can also provide details of city walk tours and coach tour operators in their area. They can assist with itineraries and may arrange bookings for you, possibly for a nominal fee. Guided tours and excursions can also be booked through your hotel reception in most resort areas and large cities, and through numerous travel agencies (*agencia de viaje*). Check at the time of booking that your courier will be able to speak your language.

L

LANGUAGE (See Useful Expressions on the inside front cover of this guide)

The national language of Spain is Castilian and it is understood

throughout the country, though inhabitants of the Basque Country,

Galicia, Catalonia and the Balearics speak Euskara, Gallego, Catalan and dialects of Catalan respectively.

Even if you learned Spanish (Castilian) at school, you might find the local accent a little difficult to understand at first. However, in main resort areas and cities, locals usually speak a certain amount of English, also German, French and Italian.

The Berlitz SPANISH PHRASE BOOK AND DICTIONARY covers most situations you are likely to encounter. It is polite to learn at least a few basic phrases and useful expressions such as those listed below:

	Castilian	Catalan
Good morning/day.	**Buenos días.**	**Bon dia.**
Good afternoon/evening.	**Buenas tardes.**	**Bona tarda.**
Good night.	**Buenas noches.**	**Bona nit.**
Please...	**Por favor...**	**Si us plau...**
Thank you.	**Gracias.**	**Gràcies.**
You're welcome.	**De nada.**	**De res.**
Goodbye.	**Adiós.**	**Adéu.**

where/when/how	**dónde/cuándo/cómo**
How much?	**¿Cuanto?**
yesterday/today/tomorrow	**ayer/hoy/mañana**
day/week/month/year	**día/semana/mes/año**
left/right	**izquierda/derecha**
up/down	**arriba/abajo**
good/bad	**bueno/malo**
big/small	**grande/pequeño**
hot/cold	**caliente/frío**
old/new	**viejo/nuevo**

LOST PROPERTY (*objetos perdidos*) (See CRIME on p.154)

Check with hotel reception before you report a missing item to the Municipal Police or Guardia Civil (see POLICE on p.166). They will issue you with a form which you will need a copy of if you wish to make an insurance claim once you are home. For items left behind on public transport, ask your hotel receptionist to telephone the bus or train station or taxi company.

I've lost my wallet.   **He perdido mi cartera.**

handbag/passport   **bolso/pasaporte**

MEDIA

Radio and Television (*radio y televisión*). Night reception is generally good enough to hear most European countries on medium-wave transistor portables, including the BBC World Service and Voice of America. Network television programmes are all in Spanish. However, the better hotels also have satellite TV with CNN, MTV and Superchannel.

Newspapers and Magazines (*periódicos y revistas*). In major tourist areas you can buy most European newspapers on the day of publication, but at about three times the price. British and American magazines are also available. The weekly English-language newspaper, the *Iberian Daily Sun*, is published in Madrid. On the Costa del Sol, *Sur* provides a round-up of local news and events for English-speaking residents and visitors.

MEDICAL CARE (See also EMERGENCIES on p.158)

EU residents should obtain form E111 which entitles them to free medical treatment within the EU. It is unwise to travel without health insurance as treatment can be expensive.

Many visitors from northern climes often suffer painful sunburn through overdoing it on the first day or two. Take the sun in short doses for at least the first few days. Go steady on alcohol as well. Cheap spirits are poured in liver-destroying measures, and beer and *sangría* also pack a punch, especially when combined with the heat. Drink plenty of bottled water (*agua mineral*) to avoid dehydration.

A list of doctors who speak your language is available at local tourist offices. There are hospitals in all principal towns and a first-aid station (*casa de socorro*) in smaller places.

Chemists (*farmacia*) are easily recognizable by a green cross sign, and are open during normal shopping hours. After hours, at least one per town – the *farmacia de guardia* – remains open all night. Its location is posted in the windows of other *farmacias*.

MONEY MATTERS

Currency. The monetary unit of Spain is the *peseta* (pta). Coins come in 1, 5, 10, 25, 50, 100, 200 and 500 pta denominations. Bank-notes come in 1,000, 2,000, 5,000 and 10,000 pta denominations.

Banking hours are usually from 8.30am to 2pm Monday-Friday. Some banks in popular resort areas also open for longer hours and on Saturdays at the height of the season. Beware of the hefty transaction charges and take your passport with you when changing money or traveller's cheques.

Outside banking hours, many travel agencies display a *cambio* sign and will change foreign currency. Most hotels will also change money, but the rate is likely to be poor. City department stores, such as *El Corte Inglés*, sometimes provide a currency exchange service. Some banks are also equipped with hole-in-the-wall bill changing machines which operate 24 hours a day. They will exchange foreign banknotes for Spanish currency. But, again, the exchange rate is likely to be unattractive.

Traveller's cheques always get a better rate than cash.

Credit cards, traveller's cheques and **Eurocheques** are accepted in most hotels, restaurants and big shops.

Planning your budget

The following list will give you some idea of prices in Spain. Prices continually change however, and while these were correct at the time of going to press, they must be regarded as approximate and vulnerable to inflation.

Attractions. Water parks: 1,600 pta per adult, 1,000 pta per child.

Babysitters. From 750 pta per hour.

Beach equipment. Two sun beds and a sunshade 1,000-1,400 pta per day.

Bicycle hire. From 900 pta for a push-bike/1,300 pta for a mountain bike per day.

Camping. High season average per day: site – 2,000 pta; tent – 450 pta; adult – 450 pta; child – 400 pta.

Car hire. Rates vary widely. The following is an average of local companies. Group A (*Seat Marbella*) 1-3 days – 3,800 pta per day; 7 days – 21,000 pta. Group B (*Ford Fiesta/Renault Twingo*) 1-3 days – 4,000 pta per day; 7 days – 24,000 pta. Group C (*Renault Clio/Ford Escort*) 1-3 days – 5,100 pta per day; 7 days – 30,800 pta.

Excursions. Half-day Barcelona City Highlights tour 3,800 pta; full-day coach tour to Toledo from Madrid (including museum entrance fees and a meal) 7,500 pta.

Hotels (double room with bath/shower, low to high season). There are great variations from city to city and resort to resort. 5-star 25,000 pta plus (add 15 per cent tax); 4-star 8,500-25,000 pta (add 6 per cent tax, or 4 per cent in the Canaries, to all other categories of hotel); 3-star 6,000-20,000 pta; 2-star 4,500-8,000 pta.

Meals and drinks. Continental breakfast from 500 pta; *menu del día* from 1,000 pta; three-course lunch/dinner (excluding wine) in a fairly good establishment, around 2,700 pta. Coffee from 125 pta; beer (local) from 125 pta; soft drinks from 150 pta.

Motorway (*autopista*) **tolls**. Sample tolls: Seville–Jerez de la Frontera (67km/41 miles) expect to pay about 895 pta; La Junquera (French border)–Barcelona (158km/98 miles) 1,530 pta; San Sebastián–Burgos (250km/154 miles) 2,960 pta.

Museums. 250-600 pta on average. Free to under 18s and over 65s; 50 per cent student concessions.

Nightlife. Discothéque admission from 600 pta (includes first drink); casino admission 550 pta.

Petrol. Average price per litre: super, 113 pta; lead free (*sin plomo*), 107 pta; diesel (*gasóleo*), 87 pta.

Shopping. Bread (250g) 70 pta; butter (250g) from 250 pta; pork/veal (per kilo) 700-1,200 pta; instant Nescafé coffee (200g) 680 pta; bottle of wine from 220 pta; fruit juice (1 litre) from 200 pta; milk (1 litre) from 100 pta.

Sports. *Golf*: green fee 4,500-7,000 pta per day; club hire from 2,000 pta. *Horseriding*: from 1,200 pta per hour. *Tennis*: from 500 pta per hour. *Waterskiing*: 10,000 pta per hour. *Windsurfing*: 1,500 pta per hour. *Parascending*: 3,500 pta. '*Water sausage*': 600 pta.

Taxis. Flat charge of 170-260 pta, plus approximately 80 pta per kilometre. Additional charges for baggage, trips to the airport and journeys on holidays, Sundays and after midnight.

OPENING HOURS (See also PUBLIC HOLIDAYS on p.167)

These vary, but generally plan to work around the siesta when whole towns and villages literally pack up and go to bed for a sleep during the mid-afternoon.

Banks. 8.30am-2pm Monday to Friday.

Bars and restaurants. It is difficult to generalize, but most bars are open from noon (or earlier) until the small hours. Restaurants serve lunch 1-4pm, and dinner 8.30-10.30pm or 11pm.

Museums. Times are variable, but most open between 10am and 1 or 2pm, and re-open 4pm-6 or 7pm. However, some do remain open over the siesta. Most museums close one day a week, generally on a Monday.

Post offices. As a rule, 8am-noon and 5-7.30pm Monday-Friday, and mornings – only on Saturday.

Shops. 9am-1pm and 4 or 5pm to 7 or 8pm Monday-Saturday. Some shops close at lunchtime on Saturdays. Department stores are generally open 10am-8pm Monday to Saturday.

PHOTOGRAPHY and VIDEO

All popular brands and types of film (*carrete*), camera and flash batteries (*pila*), and general accessories are widely available, but may cost rather more than they do at home. Processing and developing in Spain is expensive.

Photography is forbidden in some churches and museums. Field workers, fishermen and peasant farmers can make very photogenic subjects but, wherever possible, ask for their permission before you take their picture. Most do not mind and are often quite amused, but respect older folk who turn away.

It is forbidden to take photographs of any military bases, military or naval port areas, police, government or military personnel.

For handy tips on how to get the most out of your holiday photographs, try the Berlitz-Nikon POCKET GUIDE TO TRAVEL PHOTOGRAPHY (available in the UK only).

I'd like a film for this camera.	**Quisiera un carrete para esta máquina.**

POLICE (*policía*)

There are three police forces in Spain. The best known is the *Guardia Civil* (Civil Guard), who patrol the highway in pairs on large, white motorcycles. Each town has its own *Policía Municipal* (Municipal Police) who wear a different uniform depending on the town and season, but are mostly found in blue and grey. The third force, the *Cuerpo Nacional de Policía*, a national anti-crime unit, can be recognized by their light-brown uniforms. All policemen are armed. If you need assistance you can call on any of these forces.

Where is the nearest police station?	**¿Dónde está la comisaria más cercana?**

PUBLIC HOLIDAYS (*fiesta*)

In addition to the following Spanish national holidays, there are numerous local *fiestas* celebrated in towns and villages throughout the country at all times of the year. Check with the local tourist office for further details.

January 1	*Año Nuevo*	New Year's Day
January 6	*Epifanía*	Epiphany
May 1	*Día del Trabajo*	Labour Day
June 24	*Día de San Juan*	St John's Day (King's Name-Saint Day)
July 25	*Santiago Apóstol*	St James' Day
August 15	*Asunción*	Assumption
October 12	*Día de la Hispanidad*	Discovery of America Day (Columbus Day)
November 1	*Todos los Santos*	All Saints' Day
December 6	*Día de la Constitución Española*	Constitution Day
December 25	*Navidad*	Christmas Day
December 26	*San Esteban*	St Stephen's Day
Moveable dates:	*Viernes Santo*	Good Friday
	Lunes de Pascua	Easter Monday
	Corpus Christi	Corpus Christi
	Inmaculada Concepción	Immaculate Conception (normally December 8)

RELIGION

The national religion is Roman Catholicism. Mass is said in almost all churches. In the main tourist centres, services are also held in foreign languages. There are Protestant churches and Jewish synagogues in most major cities, but services will still be held in Spanish unless there is a significant resident English-speaking contingent in town (i.e. on the Costa del Sol).

TIME DIFFERENCES

Spanish time coincides with that of most of Western Europe – Greenwich Mean Time plus one hour. In spring, clocks are put forward one hour (in autumn they go back), maintaining the one-hour difference.

Summer Time Chart

New York	London	**Spain**	Jo'burg	Sydney	Auckland
6am	11am	**noon**	noon	8pm	10pm

TIPPING

Since a service charge is normally included in hotel and restaurant bills, tipping is not obligatory. The following are just suggestions.

Hotel porter, per bag	100 pta
Maid, per week	200 pta
Waiter	10%
Taxi driver	10%

TOILETS/RESTROOMS

The most commonly used expression for toilets is *servicios* or *aseo*, though you may also hear or see *WC*, *water* and *retretes*. The usual signs are *Damas* for women, and *Caballeros* for men.

Public conveniences are rare, but all hotels, bars and restaurants have toilets, usually of a reasonable standard. It is considered polite to buy a coffee if you drop into a bar just to use the toilet.

TOURIST INFORMATION OFFICES (*oficina de turismo*)

Information about Spain can be obtained from the overseas branches of the Spanish National Tourist Office listed here. Most Spanish towns of a reasonable size have their own local tourist office, well-equipped with brochures, maps and leaflets.

Australia: PO Box A-625, Suite 21a, 203 Castlereagh Street, Sydney, NSW 2000; tel. (02) 264 7966.

Canada: 14th Floor, 102 Bloor Street West, Toronto, Ontario M5S 1M8; tel. (416) 961 3131/4079.

United Kingdom: 57-58 St James' Street, London SW1A 1LD; tel. (0171) 499 0901.

US: 665 Fifth Avenue, New York, NY 10022; tel. (212) 759 8822; Suite 960, 8383 Wilshire Boulevard, Beverly Hills, CA 90211; tel. (213) 658 7188.

TRANSPORT

Bus services. Buses (*autobús*) are cheap, reasonably comfortable and reliable in most areas, but beware of drastically reduced timetables on Sundays. There are extensive bus services within major cities, but in the countryside services generally only run into and out of provincial centres – so links to smaller towns and resorts may not be possible, even if they are quite close by.

Train services. Madrid is the hub of the complicated *RENFE* (Spanish National Railways) network, which reaches out like a spider's web to most corners of the country. There is a bewildering number of different types of train (*tren*) service, from all-stops local services such as the *Tranvía* or *Omnibus* to the high-speed *AVE*, which makes the trip from Madrid to Seville in just two hours. In between, there are *Expreso* and *Rápido* long-distance expresses, and the more luxurious *Talgo*, *Electrotren* and *TER* services. These cost considerably more than the slow services, and seats should be booked in advance.

Taxis. The letters *SP* (*servicio público*) on the front and rear bumpers of a car indicate that it is a taxi. It will probably also have a green light in the front windscreen or a green sign indicating *libre* when it is available for hire. Taxis are often unmetered in tourist areas, but fares to most destinations are fixed and displayed on a **169**

board at the main taxi rank. These are reasonable by European standards, but you can check the fare in advance with the driver.

When is the next bus/train for…?	**¿A qué hora sale el próximo autobús/tren para…?**
I want a ticket to…	**Quiero un billete para…**
What's the fare to…?	**¿Cuánto es la tarifa a…?**
first/second class	**primera/segunda clase**
single (one-way)	**ida**
return (round-trip)	**ida y vuelta**

TRAVELLERS WITH DISABILITIES

In general, the provisions for wheelchair travellers in Spain are not particularly good. There are wheelchair ramps at airports, and many larger apartment blocks and hotels do make provision for guests with disabilities. Some of the more forward-thinking resorts also provide ramp access to pavements.

Further details of accessible accommodation are given in *Holidays and Travel Abroad* published by RADAR, 250 City Road, London EC1V 8AF; tel. (0171) 250 3222. British travellers can also contact the Holiday Care Service (tel. (01293) 774535), who are experts in the field of holidays for people with disabilities.

Other sources of information are the Spanish National Tourist Office (see Tourist Information Offices on p.168), and the Federation ECOM, Gran Vía de las Corts Catalanes 562-2a, 08011 Barcelona, a group of private organizations for people with disabilities.

TRAVELLING TO SPAIN

By Air (See also Airports on p.151). Madrid receives direct transatlantic flights from New York, Miami and Montreal, as well as services from most major European cities, the Middle East and Africa. There are onward connections from Madrid to all other important Spanish cities. Iberia is the Spanish national carrier and offers the greatest choice of direct flight destinations as well as worthwhile **170** special deals.

Approximate flying times are: London–Madrid or Barcelona 2 hours; London–Málaga 2.75 hours; London–Canary Islands 4 hours; New York–Madrid 6.5 hours; New York–Barcelona 8 hours; Montreal–Madrid 7.5 hours.

For access to the *costas*, regular and inexpensive charter flights from overseas serve the regional airports of Reus (for Tarragona and the Costa Dorada), Gerona (Costa Brava), Alicante (Costa Blanca), Almería (Costa del Almería), and Málaga (Costa del Sol), as well as the Balearic and Canary Islands.

By Boat. Brittany Ferries operate a Portsmouth–Santander service during winter (crossing time 30-33 hours), and a Plymouth–Santander route for the rest of the year (crossing time 24 hours). P&O operate a year-round Portsmouth–Bilbao service (crossing time 28-29 hours).

By Road. Express coaches take 26 hours to travel from London to Barcelona, departing most days in summer. Three times a week they continue as far south as Alicante, stopping at some large towns *en route*. You can also catch a coach to Madrid, Zaragoza, Santander, Santiago de Compostela and Algeciras (contact Eurolines (0171) 730 8235 for further details).

If you are driving down through France, the main route to the west of the Pyrenees (via Bordeaux) takes you across the border at Irún, then San Sebastián, Burgos, Madrid and south. From Perpignan in southeast France, the highway continues via Barcelona to Alicante. Allow two to three days of steady driving.

By Rail. Travellers from the UK first need to make their way to Paris (3 hours by tunnel or 6-7 by boat-train). The Paris–Madrid service, for onward connections to the south (about 26 hours Paris-Málaga) and west, crosses the border at Irún; use the Paris-Barcelona service (about 12 hours) for connections to the east. The Spanish National Tourist Office can give you details on discounted fares within Spain. *Inter-Rail Cards* and *Eurail Passes* are valid on the Spanish rail network, but you may have to pay a supplement for travel on certain classes of train.

WATER (*agua*)

Although the tap water is safe to drink, it is not recommended for its taste. The Spanish themselves almost invariably drink bottled water (*agua mineral*).

WEIGHTS and MEASURES

For fluid and distance measures, see p.157.

Length

Weight

grams | 0 100 200 300 400 500 600 700 800 900 1 kg
ounces | 0 4 8 12 1 lb 20 24 28 2 lb

Temperature

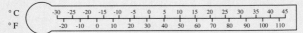

YOUTH HOSTELS (*albergues de juveniles*)

These are fairly few and far between, but you can get a list of Spanish youth hostels from the YHA or Spanish National Tourist Office. When there is nothing available, look for a *fonda*, the most basic type of accommodation (see ACCOMMODATION on p.150). *Fondas* provide fairly spartan conditions, but many enjoy convenient town-centre locations. Some have rooms with three or four beds which are **172** a bargain if you're travelling in a group.

A Selection of Hotels and Restaurants in Spain

Recommended Hotels

Below is a selection of accommodation in towns, cities and resorts throughout Spain. It is always advisable to book well in advance, particularly if you will be visiting in high season or during an important *fiesta* period.

As a basic guide to room prices, we have used the following symbols (for a double room with bath/shower during high season), but do note that you can frequently negotiate prices for more than one night, and out of high season room rates can fall sharply:

▯▯▯▯	above 20,000 pta
▯▯▯	15,000-20,000 pta
▯▯	7,000-14,000 pta
▯	below 7,000 pta

ÁVILA

Palacio Valderrábanos ▯▯
Plaza de la Catedral, 9
Tel. 21 10 23; fax 25 16 91
A historic building furnished in grand style. Ask for a room with a cathedral view, or room 229 in the old watch tower. 73 rooms.

BARCELONA

España ▯▯
Sant Pau, 9-11
Tel. 318 17 58; fax 317 11 34
An architectural gem, the España is a must if you are looking for atmosphere. Come for a meal in the

splendid Moderniste restaurant. This hotel has 84 rooms.

Gran Hotel Calderón ▯▯▯▯
Rambla de Catalunya, 26
Tel. 301 00 00; fax 317 31 57
Modern high-rise tower offering stunning views over the whole city. Indoor and outdoor pools, plus sauna and exercise rooms. 244 rooms.

Gran Vía ▯▯
Gran Vía de les Corts
Catalanes, 642
Tel. 318 19 00; fax 318 99 97
A delightful 19th-century town house. The public rooms are richly

furnished and decorated with Art Nouveau fittings. 48 rooms.

BILBAO

Villa de Bilbao ▥▥▥▥▥
Gran Vía, 87
Tel. 441 60 00; fax 441 65 29
Centrally located, with a good Basque restaurant. 142 rooms.

CÁDIZ

Francia y Paris ▥▥
Plaza de San Francisco, 2
Tel. 22 23 48; fax 22 24 31
Recently renovated *belle-époque* hotel located on a popular traffic-free plaza. 69 rooms.

CÓRDOBA

Gonzalez ▥▥
Manríquez, 3
Tel. 47 98 19; fax 48 61 87
Family hotel in part of a 16th-century palace. Public areas full of antiques. Most rooms look on to an Arab-style patio. 16 rooms.

GRANADA

Alhambra Palace ▥▥▥▥
Peña Partida, 2
Tel. 22 14 68; fax 22 22 64
Extravagant neo-Moorish creation enjoying views over Granada and the Sierra Nevada from the Alhambra hill. Gardens, terrace. 273 rooms.

América ▥▥
Real de la Alhambra
Tel. 22 74 71; fax 22 74 70
A family-run hotel within the Alhambra compound. Small rooms; vine-covered patio dining area. Excellent value for its position. 13 rooms.

GUADALUPE

Hospedaría del Real ▥
Monasterio
Plaza Juan Carlos I
Tel. 36 70 00; fax 36 71 77
Many of the bedrooms in the monastery's own hotel are converted from 16th-century monks' cells, set around a delightful courtyard. 40 rooms.

LEÓN

Parador San Marcos ▥▥▥
Plaza San Marcos, 7
Tel. 23 73 00; fax 23 34 58
Housed in a 16th-century former convent (now a national monument), this is one of Spain's finest and most luxurious *paradores*. Ask for a room in the atmospheric old part with its tapestry-lined walls. 253 rooms.

175

MADRID

Arosa   ▯▯▯
Calle de la Salud, 21
Tel. 532 16 00; fax 531 31 27
Good central location off Gran Vía. Rooms range from the grand, old style of the original building to sleek, modern quarters. Swimming pool. No restaurant. The hotel has 126 rooms.

Palace   ▯▯▯▯
Plaza de las Cortes, 7
Tel. 429 75 51; fax 429 82 66
Sumptuous *belle-époque* building with all modern comforts and a relaxed ambience. 500 rooms.

París   ▯▯
Alcalá, 2
Tel. 521 64 96; fax 531 01 88
Old favourite in a historic building in a convenient central location. 114 rooms.

MÉRIDA

Parador Vía de la Plata   ▯▯▯
Plaza de la Constitución, 3
Tel. 31 38 00; fax 31 92 08
Baroque-style former convent on the site of the old Roman Praetorian Guard Palace. Friendly management. Good regional food, pleasant bar and garden. 82 rooms.

OVIEDO

De la Reconquista   ▯▯▯▯
Gil de Jaz, 16
Tel. 524 11 00; fax 524 11 66
Luxury hotel in magnificent 18th-century building. Stylishly furnished with antiques. 142 rooms.

PAMPLONA

Avenida   ▯▯▯
Avenida de Zaragoza, 5
Tel. 24 54 54; fax 23 23 23
Charming renovated building with balconies overlooking the fountain on Plaza Príncipe de Viana. 24 rooms.

SALAMANCA

Monterrey   ▯▯▯
Azafranal, 21
Tel./fax 21 44 00
Old-world elegance, if a little faded, in the heart of the city. 89 rooms.

SAN SEBASTIÁN

María Cristina   ▯▯▯▯
Paseo de la República
Argentina, 4
Tel. 42 49 00; fax 42 39 14
This *belle-époque* beauty is the finest hotel in San Sebastian. Liveried doormen will greet you and

there is an excellent restaurant. 139 luxurious rooms.

Niza ‖

Zubieta, 56
Tel. 42 66 63; fax 42 66 63
Owned by a renowned Basque sculptor, it is a showcase for modern art and antiques. 41 rooms.

SANTIAGO DE COMPOSTELA

Los Reyes Católicos ‖‖‖‖

Plaza del Obradoiro, 1
Tel. 58 22 00; fax 56 30 94
Magnificent *parador* at right-angles to the cathedral. Founded in 1499, it claims to be the world's oldest hotel. Public rooms resemble museums; bedrooms surround quiet patios. 136 rooms.

Peregrino ‖‖‖

Avenida Rosalía de Castro
Tel. 52 18 50; fax 52 17 77
Comfortable hotel 1km (½ a mile) from the city centre. Pool, garden, terrace, views. 148 rooms.

SEGOVIA

Las Sirenas ‖

Juan Bravo, 30
Tel. 43 40 11; fax 43 06 33
A charming, if faded, 1950s hotel. Quiet, central location. 39 rooms.

Parador de Segovia ‖‖‖

Crta. de Valladolid
Tel. 44 37 37; fax 43 73 62
Ultra-modern *parador* with contemporary artworks as well as furnishings, plus superb views of Segovia from all the rooms. Indoor and outdoor pools, garden, terrace. 113 rooms.

SEVILLE

Alfonso X111 ‖‖‖‖ +

San Fernando, 2
Tel. 422 28 50; fax 421 60 33
The haunt of royals and film stars, this opulent palace was built in 1909-29. Offers every facility including swimming pool, garden and terrace. 149 rooms.

Becquer ‖‖‖‖

Reyes Cátolicos, 4
Tel. 422 89 00; fax 421 44 00
A well-equipped, modern hotel in a good central location. 120 rooms

Murillo ‖

Lope de Rueda, 7
Tel. 421 60 95; fax 421 96 16
Although the hotel has plain bedrooms, there is an old-curiosity-shop feel with antiques and unusual *objets d'art* concealed behind an ordinary town house façade in the heart of the Barrio de Santa Cruz. 57 rooms.

177

SITGES

El Xalet   ▯▯
Isla de Cuba, 33-35
Tel./fax 894 55 79
A gorgeous late 19th-century Moderniste building. Antique furnishings, air-conditioning and all the mod cons in the bedrooms. Charming period dining room, plus swimming pool and garden. 11 rooms.

Romántic   ▯▯
Sant Isidre, 33
Tel. 894 83 75; fax 894 63 01
Three 19th-century villas have been combined to form a gem of a hotel in the quiet back streets. Tiles, sculptures, wicker and greenery blend Modernism with old Cuba in the public areas and there's a delightful garden and bar. Traditionally furnished rooms. 55 rooms.

TARRAGONA

Marina   ▯
Vía Augusta, 151
Tel. 23 30 27; fax 23 33 09
Small, modern establishment with leafy front garden, resembles a private house. Modest, clean rooms plus terrace, tennis court. Conveniently placed for the Platja de l'Arabassada. 26 rooms.

TOLEDO

Cardenal   ▯▯
Paseo de Recaredo, 24
Tel. 22 49 00; fax 22 29 91
A beautifully converted 18th-century bishop's palace, now home to Toledo's most distinctive hotel. Very stylish bedrooms. 27 rooms.

La Almazara   ▯
Ctra. de Cuerva km 3.5
Tel. 22 38 66
Delightful hilltop country retreat. Many personal touches give a cosy, welcoming atmosphere to this 16th-century house. 21 rooms.

Parador Conde de Orgaz   ▯▯▯
Cerro del Emperador
Tel. 22 18 50; fax 22 51 66
Fine re-creation of a medieval country house with attractive bedrooms, 20 of which enjoy wonderful views over the city (as does the restaurant). Swimming pool and terrace. 77 rooms.

TORTOSA

Parador Castillo de la Zudo   ▯▯
Castillo de la Zuda
Tel. 44 44 50; fax 44 44 58
Marvellously restored medieval castle in a majestic position which

overlooks the town and Ebro valley. Public areas are rather gloomy, but bedrooms are decorated in comfortable local rustic style. Swimming pool. 82 rooms.

TOSSA DE MAR

Diana   ▐▐
Plaza de España, 6
Tel. 34 18 86; fax 34 11 03
The chief attraction of this charming town house is the stamp of Antoni Gaudí, who designed many of its features. Recently refurbished and very stylish. 21 rooms.

ÚBEDA

Parador Condestable   ▐▐▐
Dávalos
Plaza de Vázquez de Molina, 1
Tel. 75 03 45; fax 75 12 59
A magnificent 16th to 17th-century palace with a stunning glassed-in patio. Attention to detail is evident in the design of the public rooms and bedrooms. A friendly, lively atmosphere. 31 rooms.

VALENCIA

Excelsior   ▐▐
Barcelonina, 5
Tel. 351 46 12; fax 352 34 78
A charming old hotel with lots of character. Gleaming brass and

wood fittings, pleasant bedrooms. Central location. 65 rooms.

VALLADOLID

Imperial   ▐▐
Peso, 4
Tel. 33 03 00; fax 33 08 13
Comfortable hotel in a 16th-century former palace. Central location. 81 rooms.

Olid Meliá   ▐▐▐▐
Plaza de San Miguel, 10
Tel. 35 72 00; fax 33 68 28
A good choice in the city centre, albeit quite a functional chain hotel. Central location. 211 rooms

ZARAGOZA

Paris   ▐▐▐▐
Pedro María Ric, 14
Tel. 23 65 37; fax 22 53 97
A good, modern hotel with all facilities, recently renovated and decorated. Central location. 62 rooms.

Sauce   ▐▐
Espoz y Mina, 33
Tel. 39 01 00; fax 39 85 97
Hotel Sauce is in a charming, whitewashed house, lovingly and tastefully decorated with stylish and cosy bedrooms. Café, no restaurant. 20 rooms.

179

BALEARIC ISLANDS

IBIZA

Hostal El Corsario   ▯▯

Poniente, 5, Ibiza Town
Tel. 30 12 48
The Hostal El Corsaro is a characterful, rather Bohemian sort of place decorated in old Ibiza style. Some of the rooms have antique fittings. There is a pleasant terrace. 14 rooms.

Hacienda Na   ▯▯▯▯
Xamena

San Miguel
Tel. 33 45 00; fax 33 45 14
The Hacienda Na Xamenda is the island's most luxurious hotel in a peaceful hillside setting with wonderful views. The hotel is decorated in a traditional Ibicenco style and has grand bedrooms. There are 54 rooms.

MAJORCA

La Residencia   ▯▯▯▯

Son Moragues, Deiá
Tel. 63 90 11; fax 63 93 70
La Residencia is a well-known country house hotel set in gorgeous gardens. Service and rooms are impeccable. The hotel has a pool, terraces and outstanding **180** restaurant. 27 rooms.

Mar y Vent   ▯▯

Calle Mayor, 49, Banyalbufar
Tel. 61 80 00; fax 61 82 01
A charming, friendly, family-run hotel with splendid views of the coast and hillside terraces. Homelike décor including antiques and hand-carved beds. 30 rooms.

Son Vida   ▯▯▯▯

Son Vida
Tel. 79 00 00; fax 79 00 17
The core of this deluxe hotel is a 13th-century castle in a magnificent setting. Antiques abound. Three pools, tennis courts, adjacent golf course. 165 rooms.

MINORCA

Hostal Biniali   ▯▯

Crta. S'Vestra, 50, San Luis
Tel. 15 17 24; fax 15 03 52
Old country house with a homelike feel and friendly management. The rooms are decorated with antiques. Excellent views, swimming pool, garden, superb restaurant. 9 rooms.

Port Mahón   ▯▯▯▯

Avenida Fort de l'Eau, Mahón
Tel. 36 26 00; fax 35 10 50
Modern hotel overlooking the port. Friendly welcome, traditional furnishings, pretty bedrooms. Swimming pool. 74 rooms.

CANARY ISLANDS

FUERTEVENTURA

Conde de la Gomera   ▮▮▮▮
Parador
Balcón de la Villa y Puerto
la Gomera
Tel. 87 11 00; fax 87 11 16
This comfortable country manor is
beautifully furnished and enjoys a
breathtaking cliff-top site with
panoramic views. 42 rooms.

Parador de   ▮▮
Fuerteventura
Playa Blanca, 48
Tel. 85 11 50; fax 85 11 58
Modern, low-rise hotel right on
the ocean front. 50 rooms.

GRAN CANARIA

Club de Mar   ▮▮
Playa de Mogán, Puerto Morgán
Tel. 56 50 66; fax 74 02 23
Situated in a mini-village of hotels
and apartments around the lovely
Puerto Mogán marina, and de-
signed to blend in with local style.

Santa Catalina   ▮▮▮▮
León y Castillo, 227, Las Palmas
Tel. 24 30 40; fax 24 27 64
Beautiful historic building patronized by Spanish and British royalty. The Santa Catalina enjoys a
splendid leafy position in the Parque Doramas. 208 rooms.

LANZAROTE

Los Fariones   ▮▮▮
Acatife, 2, Urb. Playa Blanca,
Puerto del Carmen
Tel. 51 01 75; fax 51 02 02
Long-established hotel located on
the best part of this fine beach with
a secluded cove and luxurious
palm garden in the grounds. Quiet
atmosphere despite central location. 237 rooms.

TENERIFE

Mencey   ▮▮▮▮
Avenida Dr José Naveiras, 38,
Santa Cruz
Tel. 27 67 00; fax 28 00 17
The Mencey is probably the finest
hotel in the Canary Islands and on
a par with the world's great hotels.
Patios and balconies, antiques and
art. 298 rooms.

Monopol   ▮▮
Quintana, 15, Puerto de la Cruz
Tel. 38 46 11; fax 37 03 10
A charming, characterful, old family-run establishment in the town
centre. Simple, modern facilities
plus balconied façade, tropical-
style patio as well as rooftop pool.
There are 100 rooms.

181

Recommended Restaurants

It is advisable to book in advance for dinner at all establishments during the high season. Many restaurants offer cheaper fixed-price menus in addition to their à la carte choices, so do not be put off a restaurant if the prices seem just out of your range. To give you an idea of the price for an *à la carte* three-course meal per person without wine we have used the following symbols:

▊▊▊▊	over 4,500 pta
▊▊▊	3,500-4,500 pta
▊▊	2,500-3,500 pta
▊	under 2,500 pta

ÁVILA

Méson del Rastro ▊▊
El Rastro, 1
Tel. 21 12 18
Simple Castilian home-cooking in a large, country-style dining room. Lively, friendly atmosphere, particularly at lunchtime.

BARCELONA

Botafumeiro ▊▊▊▊
Major de Gràcia, 81
Tel. 218 42 30
Perfectly presented and prepared fish and shellfish dishes from Galicia; reputedly the best restaurant serving this type of cuisine in Barcelona. The Botafumeiro is closed on Sunday evening and the whole day Monday.

Los Caracoles ▊▊–▊▊▊
Escudellers, 14
Tel. 302 31 85
This restaurant *típico* is a minor legend and serves classic Catalan cuisine at reasonable prices. Cosy, rambling, old-fashioned dining rooms in the Barri Gòtic. It is patronized by opera and theatre personalities, whose signed photos adorn the walls.

Set Portes ▊▊
Passeig de Isabel II, 14
Tel. 319 30 33
A venerable institution, housed in a national monument and little altered since it opened in 1836. Extensive, reasonably priced menu of Catalan specialities. The seven dining rooms (open 1pm-1am) cater to a capacity of 1,000 diners.

BILBAO

Goizeko-Kabi ▦▦▦▦
Particular de Estraunza, 4
Tel. 442 11 29
One Michelin rosette for its roasted woodcock with Armagnac and the *bacalao* (cod). Closed Sunday.

CÁDIZ

El Faro ▦▦▦
San Félix, 15
Tel. 22 13 20
Specialises in splendid fish dishes and Andalusian cooking is the forté of this highly regarded and popular establishment.

CÓRDOBA

Almudaina ▦▦▦
Jardines de los Santos Mártires, 1
Tel. 47 43 42
Situated in a 15th-century Andalusian building with patio, this excellent restaurant specializes in local produce and unusually interesting vegetable dishes. Outdoor seating. Closed Sunday evening.

El Churrasco ▦▦▦
Romero, 16
Tel. 29 08 17
Córdoba's most famous restaurant. Try the *churrasco* (a grilled pork dish with hot pepper sauce),

or *dorada* baked in salt. Outdoor dining. Closed August.

GRANADA

El Amir ▦▦
General Narváez, 3
Tel. 26 68 18
Well-known for its Moorish and North African dishes. Unassuming surroundings, but warm welcome in the lower town.

Mirador de Morayma ▦▦▦
Callejón de las Vacas
Tel. 22 82 90
Romantic Andalusian restaurant in the old Albaicín district. Great views over the city. Closed Sunday evening and Monday.

MADRID

Botín ▦▦▦
Cuchilleros, 17
Tel. 366 42 17
Possibly the world's oldest restaurant, established in 1725. Traditional roasts are the speciality.

Casa Lucio ▦▦▦
Cava Baja, 35
Tel. 365 32 52
Very upscale *tapas* bar. Try the *churrasco de la casa* (a huge sizzling steak). Closed Saturday lunchtime and August.

183

El Cenador del Prado ▌▌▌▌
Prado, 4
Tel. 429 15 61
Excellent *nueva cocina* in one of the city's most outstanding restaurants. One Michelin rosette. Closed Saturday lunchtime, Sunday, and 2 weeks August.

Zalacaín ▌▌▌▌
Alvarez de Baena, 4
Tel. 561 48 40
Spain's finest restaurant according to many critics. Winner of three Michelin stars for its international and Basque-Navarrese-style cuisine. Closed Saturday lunchtime and Sundays, and in August.

PAMPLONA

Shanti ▌▌
Castillo de Maya, 39
Tel. 23 10 04
Good local cooking and reasonable prices. Closed Sunday and Monday evenings, and July.

RONDA

Don Miguel ▌▌▌
Plaza de España
Tel. 287 10 90
Ever-popular for its terrace overlooking the famous town-centre gorge, this restaurant is also noted for good Andalusian cooking.

Sample the venison and game dishes in season. Closed Sunday, Wednesday in summer, mid-January to mid-February.

SALAMANCA

Río de la Plata ▌▌▌▌
Plaza del Peso, 1
Tel. 21 90 05
Small, charming restaurant serving traditional Castilian dishes as well as seafood. Closed Monday and July.

SAN SEBASTIÁN

Arzak ▌▌▌▌
Alto de Miracruz, 2
Tel. 27 84 65
Outstanding traditional Basque cuisine served at this winner of three Michelin stars. Superb game and seafood dishes; attentive service. Closed Sunday evening, Monday, 2 weeks in June, and 2 weeks in November.

SANTANDER

Puerto ▌▌
Hernán Cortés
Tel. 21 93 93
A good restaurant specializing in delicious Cantabrian seafood dishes prepared in the open over a charcoal grill.

SANTIAGO DE COMPOSTELA

Anexo Vilas   ▯▯▯▯
Avenida de Villagarcia, 21
Tel. 59 83 87
This family-run restaurant has been serving fine Galician food for over 80 years. Closed Monday.

SEGOVIA

José María   ▯▯
Cronista Lecea, 11
Tel. 43 44 84
Traditional Castilian fare served in a lively rustic-yet-trendy atmosphere. Noisy *tapas* bar with a good selection of dishes.

SEVILLE

La Albahaca   ▯▯▯▯
Plaza de Santa Cruz, 12
Tel. 422 07 14
Charming Andalusian mansion with restrained décor serving international and regional food. Try the pumpkin soup or wild red partridge. Outdoor dining. Closed Sunday.

Figón del Cabildo   ▯▯▯
Plaza del Cabildo
Tel. 422 01 17
Both modern and traditional Andalusian dishes feature on the menu at the Figón del Cabildo, including a good choice of fish and seafood. Try the eel and endive salad. Closed Sunday.

TARRAGONA

Sol Ric   ▯▯▯
Vía Augusta, 227
Tel. 23 20 32
An excellent garden restaurant established in 1959, and a long-time favourite for its fish and shellfish dishes, as well as *romesco* specialities. Closed on Sunday evening and Monday.

Les Voltes   ▯▯
Trinquet Vell, 12
Tel. 21 88 30
Atmospheric location in the actual vaults of the old Roman circus. High-tech fittings, Spanish and international cuisine. Try the *arròs negre* (black rice).

TOLEDO

Hostal de Cardenal   ▯▯
Paseo de Recaredo, 24
Tel. 22 49 00
Traditional Spanish home-cooking, including meaty game specials, served in the beautiful surroundings of an 18th-century bishop's palace. (Same owners as the notable Botín in Madrid.)

185

VALENCIA

Les Graelles   ▌▌▌
Arquitecto Mora, 2
Tel. 360 47 00
Excellent rice dishes are the house speciality. Good service. Closed Sunday evening and August.

VALLADOLID

Mesón Cervantes   ▌▌▌
Paseo de Zorrilla, 10
Tel. 33 71 02
Excellent Castilian cuisine. Friendly, efficient service. Closed Sunday evening and August.

ZARAGOZA

La Venta del Cachirula   ▌▌▌
Crta. N232 km 4.5
Tel. 33 16 74
Typical Aragonese restaurant just north of Zaragoza. Serves regional dishes. Closed Sunday evening and 2 weeks August.

BALEARIC ISLANDS

IBIZA

La Masia d'en Sord   ▌▌
Crta. San Miguel, Ibiza Town
Tel. 31 02 28
Delightful 17th-century farmhouse with a romantic terrace and rustic dining room. Mediterranean cuisine; specialities include salmon cooked in *cava*.

Sa Cova   ▌▌
Santa Lucia, 5, Ibiza Town
The dining room enjoys an unusual setting, built into a cave with an outdoor terrace boasting views of the cathedral. Daily menu.

MAJORCA

Ca'n Quet   ▌▌▌
Crta. Deiá, Deiá
Tel. 63 91 96
Renowned restaurant which draws locals from Palma to feast on delicacies such as giant prawns wrapped in puff pastry. Quality cuisine with unique local touches. Closed Monday.

Son Tomás   ▌▌
Baronia, 17, Banyalbufar
Tel. 61 81 49
Enjoy the wonderful views from the terrace of this village restaurant while you tuck into seafood.

MINORCA

Es Plá   ▌▌ (lobster ▌▌▌▌)
Pasaje Es Plá, Fornells
Tel. 37 66 55
The island's most famous restaurant patronized by none other than

King Juan Carlos, who comes here for the *caldereta de langousta*, a delicious lobster stew. If your wallet will not accommodate the royal favourite, there are plenty of other good things to try.

Mesón El Gallo ‖

Crta. Cala Galdana km 1.5
Ferrerías
Tel. 37 30 39
Old farmhouse restaurant with a faithful clientele, specializing in Menorcan home-cooking using fresh local ingredients. Try the *paella del gallo*. Closed Monday.

CANARY ISLANDS

FUERTEVENTURA

La Molina ‖

Antigua
Canarian specialities served in an atmospheric restaurant next to the windmill.

GRAN CANARIA

El Cerdo Que Rie ‖

Paseo de las Canteras, 31
Las Palmas
The 'Laughing Pig' offers fine international and Spanish cuisine in informal, colonial-style surroundings. *Fondues* and *flambés* are house specialities.

LANZAROTE

La Era ‖

Barranco, 3, Yaiza
Tel. 83 00 16
A whitewashed courtyard decked with flowers opens onto two tiny 17th-century, rustic dining rooms, from where island specialities are served.

El Varadero ‖–‖

Varadero, 2, Puerto del Carmen
Tel. 82 57 11
Fine fish and a good selection of *tapas* are served in this atmospheric old warehouse on the harbour. Live piano music.

TENERIFE

Mario ‖‖

Edificio Rincón del Puerto
Plaza del Charco
Puerto de la Cruz
Small fish restaurant decorated with nautical memorabilia. Closed on Monday.

Mi Vaca Y Yo ‖

Cruz Verde, 3, Puerto de la Cruz
Tel. 38 52 47
Superb international food served in an exotic sub-tropical setting. A favourite tourist haunt, this restaurant serves fresh grilled fish and seafood specials.

187

Index

Where more than one reference occurs, the one in **bold** refers to the main entry. Entries in *italics* refer to illustrations.

189

190

Berlitz – pack the world in your pocket!

Africa
Algeria
Kenya
Morocco
South Africa
Tunisia

Asia, Middle East
Bali and Lombok
China
Egypt
Hong Kong
India
Indonesia
Israel
Japan
Malaysia
Singapore
Sri Lanka
Taiwan
Thailand

Australasia
Australia
New Zealand
Sydney

Austria, Switzerland
Austrian Tyrol
Switzerland
Vienna

Belgium, The Netherlands
Amsterdam
Bruges and Ghent
Brussels

British Isles
Channel Islands
Dublin
Edinburgh
Ireland
London
Scotland

Caribbean, Latin America
Bahamas
Bermuda
Cancún and Cozumel
Caribbean
Cuba

French West Indies
Jamaica
Mexico
Mexico City/Acapulco
Puerto Rico
Rio de Janeiro
Southern Caribbean
Virgin Islands

Central and Eastern Europe
Budapest
Hungary
Moscow and St Petersburg
Prague

France
Brittany
Châteaux of the Loire
Côte d'Azur
Dordogne
Euro Disney Resort
France
Normandy
Paris
Provence

Germany
Berlin
Munich
Rhine Valley

Greece, Cyprus and Turkey
Athens
Corfu
Crete
Cyprus
Greek Islands
Istanbul
Rhodes
Turkey

Italy and Malta
Florence
Italy
Malta
Milan and the Lakes
Naples
Rome
Sicily
Venice

North America
Alaska Cruise Guide
Boston
California
Canada
Disneyland and the Theme Parks of Southern California
Florida
Greater Miami
Hawaii
Los Angeles
Montreal
New Orleans
New York
San Francisco
Toronto
USA
Walt Disney World and Orlando
Washington

Portugal
Algarve
Lisbon
Madeira
Portugal

Scandinavia
Copenhagen
Helsinki
Oslo and Bergen
Stockholm
Sweden

Spain
Barcelona
Canary Islands
Costa Blanca
Costa Brava
Costa del Sol
Costa Dorada and Tarragona
Ibiza and Formentera
Madrid
Mallorca and Menorca
Seville
Spain

IN PREPARATION
Czech Republic

019/602